Rink van der Velde

the trap

Translated by Henry J. Baron

THE PERMANENT PRESS
Sag Harbor, New York 11963

Library of Congress Cataloguing-in-Publication Data

Velde, Rink van der.
  (Fûke. English)
  The Trap/by Rink van der Velde.
    p. cm.
  ISBN 1-877946-80-X
  I. World War, 1939-1945--Netherlands--Friesland--Fiction.
PF1531.V44F8913   1997
839'.234--dc20   96-27256
                                                      CIP

First Edition, February 1997 — 1200 copies

THE PERMANENT PRESS
Noyac Road
Sag Harbor, NY 11963

Foreword

Rink van der Velde was born in Friesland, a province of The Netherlands, in 1932. By profession a journalist, he has especially established himself as a first-rate story-teller among Frisian prose writers. His novels and short stories frequently feature a sociocritical dimension and attract a large readership. Critics have acclaimed *The Trap* as perhaps his best accomplishment among the more than twenty novels and numerous collections of short stories he has written since 1960. The author received the Gysbert Japiks prize in 1975, the most distinguished literary prize awarded by the Province of Friesland.

The Trap, a short war novel based on a real incident, tells the story, with utter economy, of a Frisian fisherman whose cottage on the lake becomes a refuge for those who need a hiding place. One day his only son is caught by the Germans, and the fisherman must make a choice. It is a searing and memorable tale, a classic tragedy that celebrates human courage and dignity in the face of defeat.

As have many of van der Velde's novels, *The Trap* has been translated into Dutch; it has also been translated into Ukrainian. The stage version of the novel has over the years enjoyed frequent performances and enthusiastic receptions. It is especially appropriate that fifty-two years after liberation this novel makes a new appearance, both in its revised version in Frisian and Dutch, and in its first translation into English.

***

1.
The Raid

Some people feel by intuition, but he had never had forebodings, and so he was caught off guard this time, too. He heard the rattle of the loose boards in the bridge, and when he turned around, he saw the light coming up the drive. Then the light was turned off, but the engine was not.

He had just pulled the boat on shore and stomped the stake into the ground. The latter wasn't necessary, because there was a breeze only in the middle of the lake. By the shore the water lay as flat as a mirror, frozen under the lingering fog and twilight.

He stood by the edge and had thought to himself that he could put on the tea before taking the eel out of the live box. It was cold, and there hadn't been one dead eel on the floaters, so there was time for such an indulgence.

The motorcycle coming up the drive changed his mind. He crossed the yard to the shed and opened the door. At the same time he looked past the house to the drive where it was still dark. Much darker than on the lake, which began to reflect the light.

The sound came closer and now and then there was a momentary flash of light. They didn't trust the path because of yesterday's rain. The cycle frequently got stuck, from the sound of the engine, anyway.

He hollered through the door: "Fellas, something's coming, you gotta clear out."

Cor was beside him at once, afraid and jumpy. "What is it? Are they coming? Are the Germans coming?"

"Somebody's coming, but I don't know if it's Germans."

Cor ran into the dark of the barn and grabbed his blankets. At the same time he swore at Willem, who always took longer to do things.

He said: "Wait for the girl, then you can take her along, because I have to use the small scow pretty soon."

The girl—he never called her by name—slept in the back part of the house. He grabbed the door handle and ducked down for the low-hanging rain gutter.

"Something's coming," he said. "The fellas are by the boat already."

No answer came from the dark. Feeling his way, he took a few steps and pulled on the blankets. She sat up at once.

"Something's coming," he said again.

He groped along the wall and found the kerosene lamp on the crate next to the bed.

The girl was out of bed already and grabbed his arm. "Are the Germans coming?"

Her voice was hoarse and scared and she was shaking.

"I don't know, but there's a motorcycle coming up the drive."

Then she heard the sound too. While he gave her a light, she grabbed her clothes together. She pulled the black overcoat that Germ had found for her over her long nightie and stuffed her dress and stockings into her shopping bag.

"The fellas are by the boat already, I'll clean up," he said.

Her breath came in short gasps and she stumbled over the doorstep. She gets more frightened every time, he thought.

He had wanted to ask her where Germ was, but she was already gone. He laid the blankets in place and ran around the bed to the ladder. With the lamp in one hand and the other on the top of the ladder, he lit up half the attic. The bed, one end against the ceiling, had not been slept in. He went down and took the blankets off the girl's bed after all. The soft warmth of her body met him.

That child has such a strange smell, Gryt had said once.

With the bedding under his arm he ran through the hallway. At the end, by the cellar door, he found by feel the pail in which Gryt soaked the dirty clothes. He shoved the sheet under the suds. With the blankets he went to the little room and, through the open doors of the cupboard bed, threw them over Gryt. She turned over and grumbled something but immediately dozed off again. He put the pillow on his own bed. On his way out again, he remembered that the girl would often put some of her things on the mantelpiece. He felt around and found a comb and a hairbrush. He shoved the things under the dirty wash in the pail. The lantern was still in the back part of the house. He blew out the light and set it behind the door.

The motorcycle must be halfway by now. It couldn't go very fast. The lane was in bad shape there and anyone not forewarned could easily sink up to the knees into the mud. With a motorcycle it must be even slower going. He took a few steps toward the access canal and listened. The scow had disappeared, though he could still hear the splash of the pole. Cor was pretty good at it.

To make certain, he went back to the shed, dropped to his knees, and felt around the place where the men had been sleeping. They had left nothing. He spread the straw around and threw a couple of old fish traps on top.

Then he ran back across the yard to the larger scow and dragged the dipnet through the live box. Nice bunch of eel, including some gray ones. The bobbers should be set tonight too, while the fishing was good.

Then it occurred to him that he might not get a chance to do that. It was a strange feeling. He stepped from the scow and waited.

He would have liked to know where Germ was. The boy was often gone at night, but he would usually tell them ahead of time. Yesterday at lunchtime he had said nothing. If he was on the way home, he would notice soon enough that it was not safe now.

He paced back and forth on the yard for a bit and then went back to the scow. The eel had to be taken care of.

He heard Gryt in the door. "What's coming?"

"A motorcycle, I'd say. Why don't you put the tea water on, then I'll take care of the eel. It was a good catch tonight."

But he made no effort to start and Gryt stepped into her clogs.

"Is everything cleared out?"

"Of course, otherwise I wouldn't be standing here."

He searched for some chewing tobacco. But it was too early.

He had purposely not put the pouch into his pocket, for if he started on that too early in the morning, he would be paying for it at night.

"Germ is not home," he said.

He had grabbed the dipnet and took the lid off the live box.

"He hasn't been home?"

"The bed's untouched."

He lay the dipnet on the open live box and stepped on shore.

They had reached the gate when they swung into action. All of a sudden everything was lit by powerful flashlights. They shone the lights on the front of the house and saw him standing. He could see the shadow of one man and then another, and behind the light of the motorcycle were more. They wore long coats. They began to search the yard, and two of them stopped in front of him and shined their lights in his face.

"We're expected," said one. "It's cold."

"That's from that damp mist," said the other.

An officer wearing a high officer's cap came by and kicked against the scow. He shined his flashlight on the scow and muttered something.

There must be about five or six of them, he thought. He could hear them throw the fish traps around in the shed and turn over the old tanning kettle that stood in the far corner.

The man with the cap had reached the clump of willows where he had his new tanning kettle. He looked at it from all sides and hollered something. Someone came from behind the house, also wearing a cap, and he saw that it was a policeman. Not one of the water police, he knew all of those. It had to be Bolhuis, the village policeman.

The officer asked about all the details and the policeman did his best, but his German was bad. They also checked out the oven in which he smoked eel; the policeman sniffed. The officer went on snooping elsewhere.

He hollered: "The ground is pretty soggy there and if the gentleman wants to keep his ass clean, he'd better come out this way."

The policeman quickly passed on the message and lit the way for the officer.

Daylight began to break, and the breeze, coming off the lake, chased the mist ahead of itself.

On the side of the house two men wandered around the young fruit trees and looked behind the willows he had planted to protect the apple trees from the wind.

The officer said: "Let's go into the house."

The policeman came up to him and said: "We're going to have to search the house."

Gryt stepped aside; the officer let the policeman go first. The policeman banged his head against the eaves trough, and the officer looked at it and ducked his head. But in the hallway he bumped his cap against the tile laths and swore. He let the policeman pick up his cap.

The small room seemed crowded with four persons. They shone the flashlights around and the policeman said: "You'd better light the lamp."

Gryt did, but she had trouble with it, and he took over. He took the glass off the lamp and the officer gave him light. Two soldiers rummaged around in the back of the house and went up the ladder. They stomped around in the attic so that the lamp began to shake.

"Sit down," said the officer.

He unbuttoned his leather coat and laid the cap on the table. Gryt sat down on the chair between the two cupboard beds. He himself went around the table to the cane chair in the corner between the mantelpiece and the window bench. The policeman stayed by the door.

The officer seemed to become impatient. He pulled up a chair and put his elbows on the table. The policeman watched him and waited. Gryt was probably willing to make tea, but she didn't dare initiate it. Her hands trembled.

He moved the pillow under his seat and took the box with the chewing tobacco out of the window bench. The officer, with eyes half closed, watched him take out a wad and stick it into his mouth. In the attic the two soldiers moved the bed and threw a bunch of fish traps around that he had put by the chimney to keep dry.

The policeman said: "Why don't you tell us what you have in the house?" while he looked at the officer, who nodded his approval. "What do you have to say for yourself?"

He did not answer right away. He shifted his wad. "I did not send you word that I had something to tell you," he said then.

"Why are these people up so early?" the officer wanted to know while momentarily lifting his head.

"These are fishermen folk," explained the policeman. "They have to start early in the morning." And to him: "The Oberst would like to know why you're so early."

"That's what I hear," he said.

"Oh, can you understand it?"

"I can follow it."

He could go on to explain that he had worked in Germany long enough to learn more of the language than the policeman, but he'd better keep quiet as long as nobody asked him.

A sergeant appeared in the door, clicked his heels together, and said that they had found nothing. The officer nodded. The sergeant left with the policeman. A moment later they heard the policeman talking upstairs.

He looked outside and noticed a soldier standing under the apple trees, a gun under his arm.

13

The policeman came in and asked: "How are the boarders?"

He took the can, which he used as a spittoon, off the floor. "We are mostly alone, my wife and I."

"Nobody uses those two beds, of course. And each of you has a cupboard bed. You only need one really, so the others must be for guests."

He took a step forward and looked behind the doors of the beds. "One would gather that both have been slept in."

He did not answer because no one had asked him anything, and the policeman reported that there were four beds while only one was needed.

"I see," said the officer. "Let him explain that situation."

He called the sergeant into the room and ordered him to conduct a thorough search of the yard.

"The Oberst would like to know what you need all those beds for," said the policeman.

"Haven't you explained that yet?"

"I have noticed that there are too many beds here for two people. Who sleeps here?" He pointed to the first cupboard bed.

"I sleep there."

"And that one?"

"My wife sleeps there."

He clawed around among the blankets. "So you sleep separately."

"Coffee?" the officer asked.

"Why don't you make us some coffee," the policeman said to Gryt. She was going to get up, but he said: "We don't have coffee."

"Then tea."

14

"It's too early for us. I've got to be finished with my chores first and I didn't get to that yet."

He stood up to take his jacket off. It was stuffy in the small room and he had put a sweater on before he had started out early this morning.

"I see that you don't want to cooperate. Such people always pull on the short end of the stick."

The policeman told the officer that they refused to make coffee. The officer shrugged his shoulders.

He noticed that Gryt tried to get his eye, but he looked away intentionally. He knew what she was going to say after the soldiers had left: Now what did I tell you? Our troubles are starting all over again. Why do you get involved, we have enough trouble as it is.

"And what about all those beds for boarders?"

"We have no boarders," he said.

"So those beds in the attic and in the back of the house are just for show, not to mention the extra cupboard bed."

"In the summertime it can get pretty close in the cupboard bed and then I often sleep in the back," he said.

That was true. When on his final check before turning in he'd notice that the girl had crawled in with Germ, he'd grab the blankets off the cupboard bed and take them to the back of the house. Not that it was his intention, but he would always listen to Germ and the girl talk.

"And that boy of yours sleeps in the attic, I suppose?"

He nodded. He expected that they would press for more details, but they didn't.

"Were you home during the night?"

"I was home during the night."

"You had bobbers in the boat, did I see that right?"

"I had a few bobbers out, but I don't stay with them anymore."

That was also true. He would haul in the bobbers in the morning on his way to the traps.

"Where did you have those bobbers?"

"On the other side of the channel, by the south shore.

That's where you have the soft bottom and if you're after eel . . ."

But the policeman wasn't listening anymore. He told the officer that he had been fishing on the south side of the lake. The officer wanted to know more. "Ask him what time he was there and how long."

The policeman obliged.

He hesitated. He wondered why they didn't ask about Germ since the police knew that he had a son.

"I started setting out the stuff around eight-thirty, give or take fifteen minutes either way. I usually don't carry a watch."

"Where did you start out?"

"By the access canal below Echten. I have a shutoff trapnet there and I always check that first. And then I set out the first bunch."

The officer listened with more interest now and interrupted the policeman a few times.

He had been fishing for weeks on the south side and yesterday was no different from all the other days.

"What time did you set out for home?"

"I don't know. It was dusk when I threw the last ones out. It was almost dark, I think."

"What time were you home?"

"What time was I home, Gryt?"

Gryt, who had not yet said a word, didn't know. "Same as other nights," she said then.

He added: "We don't watch the clock too closely around here."

"A lot of fishermen stay out all night," said the policeman.

"If I have five hundred bobbers out, and it's a beautiful night, I do that too sometimes," he said, "but not for the sake of a couple of hundred. Nowadays it's not really necessary anymore either."

"Why not?"

"Nothing much can go wrong; there's not much boat traffic anymore."

And he didn't have to catch a lot, for eel was expensive. He caught as much as he needed for trading purposes. Now and again he would need his tobacco, and salt for smoking fish, and silk and cotton for the fish traps.

"You noticed nothing unusual last night?"

"I don't think so. A barge came through the channel, in the direction of the Follegeast stream. I did notice that it had a load of lumber, those meter-length beams. And the police boat from De Lemmer was there, of course, at the same time as always."

He could have added that the adjutant had been looking at him through his binoculars same as always. They'd like to catch him. When he'd be fishing for bass or pike they would always check him for undersized fish. They knew he was a poacher. And they no doubt knew he had a gun and hunted ducks. They wanted to catch him, but they weren't sharp enough.

"So you noticed nothing unusual. And what time did you start out this morning?"

"Around three-thirty."

"That's early."

"It takes three quarters of an hour to get there and with no wind you don't go very fast."

"And it was still dark when you got back, we've seen that for ourselves."

"That's because of the fog; it gets light earlier usually."

"Can you find your bobbers in the dark?"

"They're all in a row."

"How many did you have out?"

"A good hundred and fifty."

"Were they in good shape this morning?"

"Yes, I've got stones attached to them."

"But what if something sails over the top of them?"

"They usually slide right under the boat. Sometimes one gets dragged off, but a fat eel can do that too."

Something had disturbed the shutoff trapnet, though. One of the sticks was crooked. And the turn-net must have got caught on the boat's keel. But nothing was broken, and the bownets had not been touched. It probably didn't mean anything. A lot of people were in hiding around the lake and they liked to venture out at night. They would visit the women or just roam around on their own.

He had no idea what they were after. The first time they had looked for the weapons that had been dropped from airplanes, some of which had landed in the lake. That time the soldiers turned the whole house upside down and had a small army check the area all around. This time they were not after weapons, for he had received no warning from the underground to set the bobbers out somewhere else.

"You live right on the lake here, and you spend every day on the water. When something happens, you'd be the first to know," said the policeman.

"It's a big lake. I can hardly look over half of it with the naked eye. And from the south side you see nothing, because there's a long strip of reeds and bulrushes. They say that's the old road, but you should know that."

"You talk a nice line, but you don't think for a minute that we believe all this," the policeman said suddenly. He didn't even look at the officer anymore; he was taking over.

"You're right here on the lake, you see and hear everything, but you know nothing."

"That's right."

"Do you happen to know there's a war going on?"

"We notice little of that around here."

Twenty years ago he wouldn't have taken this sitting down, and not even ten years ago. He nurtured a great hatred for policemen and for all men of authority, and that had not changed. But he didn't fly off the handle so easily anymore and it wasn't at all his intention to put up a fuss now. He thought about the boy, and he wanted to be as accommodating as possible. At this point he was ready to treat the men to some coffee.

"But it is wartime," said the policeman, "and don't expect us to be too civil at such a time."

"I've never been used to good treatment by you guys," he answered, and added immediately: "I've answered every question you asked me, isn't that right?"

"You didn't give the right answers."

The policeman did not ask about the boy, and that made him uneasy. It was almost light outside now. Here and there hung a fragment of remaining fog, but a breeze was now coming off the lake.

The officer got up and went out. The policeman ran after him and they whispered together in the hall. Gryt looked at him, but he kept his eye on the soldier pacing back and forth in front of the window.

The policeman came in again and said: "You'd better get your coat on."

2.
A Bad Day

By the bridge stood a gray truck, with small barred windows on both sides of its high closed box. Two policemen and a soldier stood on guard.

"Get in," said policeman Bolhuis, and he dropped the gate at the back. He pulled himself up and sat down on the bench. The three policemen joined him and then the two soldiers got in. The gate stayed down.

Two soldiers busied themselves with the motorcycle. The thing was covered with mud and the soldiers tried to clean it up as best they could. Halfway down the drive the engine quit and they had to pull the cycle with a rope to the road.

He could see the bridgekeeper's house. The shutters were closed and no one stirred. Salverda's yard also looked forsaken. Salverda had people in hiding.

He told Gryt that she should put the eel in the container, because they would not let him finish his chores first. He was allowed to take a sandwich along, but the policeman watched while Gryt prepared it. He should have told her to send a message to the eel merchant, but he had thought of it too late. Boonstra was supposed to deliver salt, for he was almost out.

He must get back to the house as soon as possible. It might get to be a warm day, and if the fish weren't taken care of, by evening the whole business would be spoiled. He would also have to repair the bownets and get some bait for the bobbers. This interruption came at a bad time, and he said so to Bolhuis.

Bolhuis just looked at him and said nothing.

One policeman sat next to him, and the other two sat opposite him. The soldiers sat on the floor in the back, leaning against the side. They were sleepy and yawned, their heads dropping to their chest. The officer must be sitting in front with the driver.

Two soldiers were pushing the motorcycle and managed to get it started. Then the truck began to move. Bolhuis closed the gate, making it almost dark inside. He watched the two policemen opposite him rolling cigarettes and heard them say to each other that it was going to turn into a nice September day.

At that moment it hit him. He said: "I'll be damned."

"What's that?" one policeman asked.

"Different men, but the same puppets," he said. "It's always been that way. You don't give a damn whether they're capitalists or fascists, you'll dance to anybody's tune."

He felt a great fury that made his hands shake, and he broke out in sweat. It was like that time in Beets, when he had yanked a military policeman off his horse and smashed his wooden shoe in pieces on the man's head; or the time when they had left the peat boss with two broken legs. Or like the incident with the forest ranger in Duurswoude—all those times when he had flown into a rage and done something that would have been better left undone.

Bolhuis grabbed his shoulder. "That's enough from you, have you gone off your rocker?"

He had heard that before too.

The other two policemen shifted.

"What kind of character is this, Bolhuis?" they asked.

"A bad one; I bet they have quite a file on him at headquarters."

And then to him: "You'd better repeat that pretty soon, then they can add that to it right away."

"I didn't quite hear it," said one policeman. "What did he say?"

Bolhuis should have let his shoulder go, then it would have passed. But now his anger grew. He said: "What kind of guys are you that you let yourself be pushed around to go on a dirty job like this. You . . ."

Then he restrained himself.

"Oh, is that the way it is," said the policeman who had not heard him.

He wanted to say more, but he thought about the boy and kept still. Bolhuis got up and fortunately released his shoulder.

"This is sure going to be held against you, man. You're going to pay dearly for this."

Then he knew that this was going to be a bad day.

He didn't want to make trouble. He wanted to get home as soon as possible, and that was worth a lot to him, much more than in the past. Above all he wanted no trouble with the police, and neither with the Germans, and he wanted nothing to do with teacher Braaksma, the man from the underground who had come around to nag him so often. Especially not with him, that pious poop with the House of Orange ribbon under the lapel of his coat. He had not resisted when he was ordered to come along. He had not even been tempted. Gryt had been frightened and had gotten the shakes, and then she started to wail. He knew what she had wanted to say to him: "What did I tell you, we're right back into misery."

She had said that as long as they had been married, but since they had been living on the lake she had less cause for it.

He took his sandwich out of his pocket and started

eating. Bolhuis looked at the bacon between the bread. "It looks to me like that's not homegrown."

"I don't do my own butchering."

"How is your business doing?"

He gave no answer. He wished he had talked with Gryt about the eel. It would be a shame if all the fish died. And the fellas could have prepared the bobbers during the day. He wanted to lay out more tonight as long as the weather was so ideal: warm in the daytime and a dark moon at night. He had also wanted to set out a two-winged trap in the drainage ditch by the old cemetery, because the sluice valve was open and some big eel might easily come through. Maybe Germ would come back in time to prepare the business for the night. They had talked about that yesterday afternoon.

But no one talked about the boy, and he didn't trust that.

"As long as we're getting into your case, we might as well take up the subject of the black market, too," said Bolhuis.

"Man, what do I care about the black market," he said. "I don't care about making a profit, all I want is to make a living."

"Of course, but it makes a difference . . ."

"I just barter a bit. I get a slab of bacon from a farmer and he gets a meal of fish from me."

"We'll discuss it pretty soon."

The truck followed the cobblestone road that led to the village. The two policemen across from him said that it was getting stuffy and took their hats off. The soldiers, ragged and dirty, were all trying to catch a wink now and their heads bobbed up and down when the truck bounced through a pothole. The sputtering motorcycle followed behind. He thought that they should have reached town about now, but it was difficult to estimate because he had never ridden the distance in a car before.

They crossed a bridge, and that had to be the canal that led to the harbor where the creamery stood. Now the truck slowed, turned left, and stopped. Bolhuis dropped the gate and jumped out.

The sun blinded him, and he stood there blinking.

"Come on out," said Bolhuis.

The soldiers stood up and stretched.

"I hope the office boy still has some tea or coffee left," said one policeman.

"Last night there was coffee, real coffee. The Germans had it with them and Bouma made two potfuls. But the people in the clerk's office probably finished it off."

He felt ill at ease when he got out. They were parked in front of the town hall, and a soldier stood guard on its stoop. More vehicles were parked here, including a motorcycle with sidecar, and next to the bike shed stood a car loaded with soldiers. No one was on the street, and the schoolyard was also empty.

He seldom came to the village. Boonstra, the eel merchant, lived there, but when he had to get a message to him, Gryt would usually stop in.

He walked up the stoop in front of Bolhuis. The man opened the door and stood aside. "Go ahead."

They came into a long white hallway with a runner on the floor. The people behind a couple of desks on one side momentarily looked up. On the other side he saw high oakwood doors with the nameplates of the mayor and the city clerk. And at the end were the wide stairs that took a turn halfway up.

He knew the way; the adjutant of the water police had

summoned him once. He didn't want to go at first, for according to his thinking, whoever wanted him should come to him. But Gryt had said that it would be better for him to meet people halfway, so he had eventually gone on Germ's bike. The adjutant had been very accommodating. He knew that game, they always started out like that. What he had really been after was information on Kuiken, who was also a fisherman but even more of a poacher. Of course, he should have told that adjutant right away what he thought of him, but he hadn't done that. He had said that he would keep an eye on Kuiken.

The two policemen went directly to the dispatch office; the soldiers stayed outside. He had not seen the officer again. Bolhuis accompanied him up the stairs. Next to the council chamber was the police bureau. The room was empty. He sat down on the bench by the wall. Bolhuis went for the telephone on the farthest desk.

"Is Liuwes there? Ask him to come up a minute. He's on duty, right?"

A moment later a young policeman entered.

"I'd like to have a real cup of coffee too," said Bolhuis.

"Then you've got to be quick."

He was a jolly fellow, whistling a tune while he took a seat behind a desk.

"I see, another one in custody. I thought we were finished. Are there still more coming?"

He looked at him.

"I don't know," he answered.

Bolhuis left. The young policeman took a cigarette out of a package that lay on the desk. He tossed him one. "You take one too, there's lots more. The Germans have plenty."

He declined, though he would have enjoyed one. The

28

cigarette fell on the floor. He was going to leave it there but then he picked it up and brought it back. When he was back on the bench he took some chewing tobacco out of his pouch.

The policeman said: "You can chew the cigarette tobacco too; it's got to be better than that tobacco of yours, anyway."

"This is good enough for me."

The policeman sauntered through the office and picked up the telephone. "Is Bolhuis there? Did he get his coffee? Good. What am I supposed to do with this man? Yes, I'll stay here, but at twelve my shift is up and then I'll have more hours in than I usually have in a whole week. Of course, you too, but I can't help that. I'm going to request two days off right away. What did you say? I don't care what the chief has to say about it."

He put the receiver down. "Can you imagine . . ."

Bolhuis hurried back in, a cup of coffee in his hand.

"The Oberst is with the mayor again and the chief is with them, too. They got the water police involved in this one, didn't they. I saw the adjutant, and that other fellow, what's his name, again. They've been out in the field all night. They got the mayor out of bed at three o'clock this morning. He's in a pretty foul mood, according to the boys."

The two of them stood in front of the window.

"What kind of character is this, Bolhuis?" the young policeman wanted to know.

"A rascal. The water police know him pretty well."

The telephone rang and Bolhuis took the message. "He's coming."

And then to him: "Come along."

They went down the stairs and were admitted to the

mayor's office. He had never seen the man before, but he knew that he had been mayor here for years. An elderly man with a round, bald head. A German officer sat next to him and the adjutant of the water police was there too.

The mayor beckoned for him to come closer. He shifted his wad and took a few steps forward.

"You know this man, adjutant?"

"'I see him almost every day, Mr. mayor."

Through the binoculars, from the back of the police boat.

It was the same sort as the one in Beetsterzwaag, this mayor. That one in Beets had four policemen around him before he began to read him the riot act. That he was the man who had incited the peat workers to strike, that he had been the ringleader this time too, and that they would teach him a lesson or two. He had said: You wouldn't dare say this if you didn't have your henchmen here. You're a yellow bastard, not worth a shit.

This one was the same kind. But he wanted no trouble. He wanted to go home and he wanted to know above all where Germ was.

"Let's make it short," the mayor began. "What is your role in this business?"

He said nothing. He didn't know what they were talking about, otherwise he would have said something.

"Well?"

"No one has told me what this is all about," he said.

"Man, I have enough trouble with the Germans. I've got to finish this business."

"I know nothing," he said.

"Now listen, we're getting nowhere this way. If I get no results this morning, then the Oberst will take over, and that will be bad news for you. They would take it out not only on you but on the whole community. As mayor I've got to prevent that. We've got to take care of this ourselves, do you understand that?"

He had nothing to say.

"We have your service record here, if one may call it that," said the mayor. "We know who you are and I don't intend to protect a man of your sort. It's going to turn out pretty bad for you if you have nothing to tell me."

He said apologetically: "I've never bothered a soul here."

"If I may," interrupted the adjutant. "I see here that you received three sentences that are far from trivial: fourteen months, three months, four weeks, and that's just a random sampling."

"I've lived here almost five years and I've never had trouble."

"That's because you've learned to become pretty sly," said the adjutant.

"I've heard that you went fishing during the night," said the mayor.

"Last night I laid out the bobbers and checked the trapnets, and this morning I picked the stuff up again."

"And you saw nothing, of course."

He didn't answer.

"I said: and you saw nothing, of course."

He said, "I saw nothing, but it makes no difference if I say that, you don't believe me anyway."

"And you didn't notice anything last night either. Even though there was a hell of a racket."

He said: "That's almost impossible. Then I should have heard something."

"That's my thinking," said the mayor."

"But it's a big lake, and if the wind is from the south-east and the noise was on the west side, it's possible that I missed it."

He really wanted to be helpful; that wasn't it. Maybe he had heard something, the noise of an engine, but not the one of the police boat. On the other hand, he had been in his first sleep, and it was hard to hear well in the cupboard bed. But he didn't have to say all that, it wouldn't make any difference. He wasn't able to say what he had heard anyway.

"What do you have to say, adjutant?"

"I've often observed people in your yard," said the adjutant. "To me it looks like an ideal place for hiding people and things like that."

"That could be."

"I can easily tell when it's you or your wife. But these were others."

"You can't reach our place with your police boat. You must be able to see far."

On the east side the water was so shallow that the police rarely ventured outside the channel, and that was quite a distance. But he knew they had powerful binoculars.

"Are you hiding anybody, and what are they up to?" the mayor wanted to know.

"Not many people come in our yard. The bakery man, every two days, once in a while the grocer, but my wife usually does the shopping herself. And the eel merchant comes often, especially when it's hot. But that's about it."

"I see," said the mayor, "you're not going to cooperate. That's up to you, but I've warned you. I'm going to ask you one more time: Who are the men of the underground who are responsible for this? You can't make me believe that you are not involved in this, as secluded as that place of yours is."

"I've nothing to do with it."

He would like to know what had happened in the night on the lake. He didn't think that the boy had been involved. He never told them much, but if there had been a weapons drop he would have let them know. But he had left no message that he wouldn't come home to sleep. He had just stayed out for the night, which he often did. He might have gone to Echten, maybe to play cards with the men in hiding there on Klaas van Houten's place. If it got too late, he'd crawl in the hay with the men. It was also possible that he was on a weapons mission. Gryt had wanted him to forbid the boy. She blamed the girl for it. She egged him on, she said. He knew it was true. She became wild as soon as she heard the word "German." And he understood why after she told him what they had done to her dad.

"All right, it's up to you," concluded the mayor after a short silence. He gave a signal to Bolhuis, who was standing in the door. The policeman took his arm.

He still wanted to say something to the mayor. He said: "This comes at a bad time. I can't just walk out, I have . . ."

"That's none of my business," said the mayor.

He opened a drawer and started looking for something. Bolhuis pulled him by the arm.

"This messing around of yours is none of my business either."

"Now, that's enough."

The mayor pointed irritably to the door and the adjutant was up at once.

It exploded inside him, but he controlled his rage. He

didn't want to give them that satisfaction. They would love to work him over, that adjutant and Bolhuis. Just like before, when he was going to attack that district judge in Beets. Three men jumped him then, and they were still beating him when he was flat on the floor with his hands behind his back.

Before he walked through the door, he broke wind so loud that it reverberated through the hall. The mayor jumped up.

"I'll be damned, you . . ."

Bolhuis gave him a shove and quickly pulled the door shut.

"You damn peasant," said the policeman.

He stood still and said: "If you touch me again, you son of a bitch, I'll kill you."

Then they rushed through the corridor and up the stairs.

Inside the office Bolhuis flared up. "If you make one more wrong move, I'll take care of you personally."

He said nothing in return. He wanted to get out of here, as soon as possible. He sat down on the bench. A day of fishing with the trammel net didn't tire him out as much as this did.

The young policeman roared when Bolhuis told him what had happened in the mayor's office.

"How do you manage that, I mean, just at the right moment when you want it. Special technique, I suppose? We used to have a guy in our unit who could fart on command too."

Bolhuis wanted to use the telephone, but the adjutant came in. Bolhuis asked: "What is the intent?" and he pointed to him.

"The mayor said they'd better take him along."

He grabbed some papers off the desk and left; Bolhuis followed him out.

"That's going to turn into an expensive fart, man," said the young policeman with a wink.

He had thought about the telephone a while ago but didn't want to ask then. Now that it looked like they had other plans for him, he'd better go ahead.

He asked: "Would you call Boonstra, the eel merchant, for me? He's got to stop by, he'll know what to do. I've got a bunch of eel waiting and they won't last in this weather."

"Does that Boonstra live here?"

"Yes, and he has a telephone. I've called him before."

The young policeman searched in the telephone book and dialed the number. He gave the message. "Who is he? I don't know, but he can sure crank out the farts."

He beckoned for him to come, and he took the telephone. He told Boonstra to come and pick up the whole bunch. The line eel too, he wouldn't get around to smoking them today anyway. And Boonstra must not forget the salt.

"That's bad timing," said Boonstra, "because I'm out of salt. But I can give you a good salt block. You'll have to cut it up yourself. If you can get by with that for a little while, I'll get the salt to you later."

It was contrary to their agreement, but he said: "All right then."

The policeman took the telephone out of his hand. "I believe my colleagues are coming."

An office clerk looked around the corner and took off again.

The young policeman laughed. "That story is going to spread through the whole building and everybody will want to know who the guy is that can let them like that.

But what I wanted to ask, do you suppose I can get some of that fish of yours pretty soon?"

"Go ahead, he said. "Go to Boonstra and tell him that I sent you and to give you a couple of pounds. I'll take care of it with him later."

The policeman rubbed his hands. "Then this is going to turn into a good day for me after all," he said. "By golly, fried fish, I don't even know how it tastes anymore. I live in the city, you see, and you can't get a thing there. And we have to be so careful as police, right?"

He had another sandwich in his pocket and he ate it now. It was getting uncomfortable in the police bureau. The sun was shining on the windows, and it must be about coffee time. But the village remained quiet. The only sounds they heard were the occasional footsteps of a clerk and the opening and closing of a door. Outside, a couple of Germans were stomping around on the stoop.

Ideal weather for pike fishing, he thought. He could've gone near that old cemetery because there was almost no wind.

The adjutant entered and Bolhuis was with him. The adjutant stood in front of him and looked long at him.

He asked: "Is something up?"

"Yes, something is up. Just follow Bolhuis."

They went outside. A motorcycle with sidecar stood ready. He had to sit in the sidecar and a soldier started the motor. Another soldier took the backseat. Then they rode out of town.

3.
Interrogation

He had taken the road to Heerenveen only a few times before; to be precise, three times. The first time was when he had gone there to make an arrangement with Poepjes, the commercial fisherman. He had taken the tram to Heerenveen and had walked the rest of the way. Poepjes hadn't asked much money for the business, so they had come to an agreement quickly. He'd paid only three hundred guilders for the old shack on the edge of the lake. Two weeks later they had been on the road to the new place with horse and wagon. Their handful of personal belongings, along with Gryt and the boy, fit easily on one wagon.

The third time he had traveled this road had been for the funeral of his father. They had lived by the lake hardly three months then. They had never been worse off because he had to learn everything from scratch and he caught but little. Besides, eel didn't bring much money in those days.

They had not let him know that the old man was sick. He only received a postcard from Hindrik that his dad would be buried on Saturday. He had attended, though he knew what they thought of him in Beets. When they emptied out the house and divided the stuff, Thomas asked about Dad's muzzle-loader.

He wanted it.

"What do you want with that," said Thomas, "you have a hunter's permit."

They meant his fishing license. He wasn't a poacher anymore, so he wouldn't dare use the muzzle-loader anyway. But in the end, he did get to take it home with him.

Before he took that job by the polder, he had tried talking it over with his dad. The old man had lost much of his wildness and was easier to get along with now. Sometimes he could even have a decent conversation.

He said to the old man: "It's easy enough for Hindrik and Thomas to talk. They have healthy kids and they'll roll through it easy enough, but for us it's always tough going. I've gotta have a steady job, otherwise we're not gonna make it."

Dad said: "If you're gonna become a slave driver in the polder, then I'm all through with you."

He also said that it didn't make sense to him at all. "Hindrik's wife Geeske is nothing but a scurvy skeleton. There's hardly any flesh on her and she's as flat as a pancake. But healthy as a spring chicken and every year another baby. You married yourself a hulk of a woman and you have only one child, and that one is always sick."

Hindrik often said that Gryt was a whiner. "You have to be firm with her. And that boy of yours, he's not gonna amount to anything either."

They had been wrong about the boy. No one could tell now that as a baby he had been sickly.

The German on the back of the motorcycle sat with his head down deep in the collar of his overcoat and sought shelter behind the back of his mate. They paid no attention to him. They had pulled the tarp tightly around him. He couldn't move an inch.

The vehicle hobbled over the rough cobblestone road. They crossed the tracks and then followed the canal in the direction of Leeuwarden. That disappointed him. He had thought they were heading for Crackstate.

He felt at home there. He knew about the place already as a boy, from his father's stories. Later Hindrik and Thomas added their tall tales. Dad said that he couldn't count the times he'd been there to sit out his punishment.

He knew nothing about Leeuwarden and it scared him a little. The big jail was there, but if you ended up there it would be for a couple of years and not for a couple of weeks or months, as in Crackstate.

He was also getting cold, though it was nice sunny weather. The people they saw along the way in the fields had taken off their coats, but the motorcycle rode fast and the wind blew so hard in his face that the tears were running down his cheeks.

On the other side of Irnsum—he saw the name on a sign—the soldier who drove shouted something to his mate and the cycle slowed. The soldier drove onto the shoulder of the road and they got off. They lit cigarettes and took a leak by a tree. He'd like to get out too; his legs were stiff and his stomach hurt from all the bumping.

He asked: "Can I get out too?"

They didn't understand him at first and he made the gestures for relieving himself. When that didn't help, he said it in German. They untied the tarp and told him not to try to escape. One soldier took his rifle off his back and put it under his arm. He walked around a bit on stiff legs and then relieved himself behind a tree. Then the soldiers snuffed their cigarettes and told him to get back in.

Twice in his life he had been to Leeuwarden. He best remembered his trip there as a boy, with Dad and Thomas and a whole bunch of people from Beets and Terwispel. It must have been a Sunday, because they didn't have to work and there was no strike either. He could still clearly recall the large meadow surrounded by a hedge of police and soldiers. He must have been about eleven then and was already working with the other boys inside the big mudscoop.

He remembered nothing of the speeches, but the scene of the police and the soldiers standing silent in a circle was vividly etched in his memory. He remembered the trip home as well, because Dad had to keep prodding him. He could hardly keep up with the group that walked along the road, in serious discussion about the meeting they had attended. Now and then they'd break out into singing their fight song, the "Marianne." And around Akkrum, Dad and the others ran into a gang from Terwispel. Dad wanted to stop for a drink, but one guy from Terwispel blocked his way and screamed: "Workers who drink don't think, and workers who think don't drink." That made Dad angry and he knocked the man out of his way.

The motorcycle crossed a pair of bridges and turned into a wide street. They stopped, but there was no prison. It looked more like a manor house with a high iron fence and a large garden with beautiful flowers and footpaths winding through it. Such mansions one might see only in Beetsterzwaag.

The door looked like a gateway, so wide and high, with steps leading up to it. A soldier stood on guard duty by the gate, and another one by the door. Behind the door was a long corridor just as in the town hall, but much wider and higher and with brown doors on both sides as far down as one could see.

One soldier stayed with him, the other disappeared behind a door. He soon returned and took him down the corridor into a bare room with a couple of benches. One soldier seated himself by the door, the other left.

He was there for maybe less than fifteen minutes. He unbuttoned his jacket, because it was a bit stuffy in the room.

Then the soldier took him to the end of the corridor and around the corner. He was led into a room where there was only one man sitting behind a huge desk. He was half hidden from view behind a palm. The room had large windows with awnings. He had never seen such an impressive room; there were no such rooms in Crackstate and in the Hall of Justice and the City Hall in Beetsterzwaag. The ceiling was white and decorated with figurines. Chandeliers with more than twenty bulbs and adorned with beads and copper hung from the ceiling. In the corner stood a statue of a nude, also in white, one knee slightly raised and one hand behind her neck.

The wallpaper was dark red with gold flowers and there were many large paintings on the wall. The carpet on the floor was so thick that he could feel his feet sink into it.

He stood in the middle of the room, in his boots, and the door closed behind him. The man behind the desk was not in uniform and he did not speak German.

He said: "So, there you are."

He came around the desk and pointed to a couple of empty chairs.

"Sit down. Maybe you want to take your coat off. It's a bit warm." The sun was right on the windows and the awnings didn't nearly keep all the heat out.

He was a good-looking man with a nice gray suit and shoes that shone like a mirror.

He let himself down in the low, leather chair and the man sat down on the other side of the low coffee table. There were cigarettes in a wooden container, and the man took one himself and then held the box out to him. "Go ahead, take one."

"I would like some chewing tobacco."

"That's fine, but I have no chewing tobacco and I can't offer you a spittoon, either."

He said it smiling. "My grandfather chewed also. It's going out of style a bit, though, isn't it. My father did it now and again, but my mother hated it. He was a common laborer too, just like you. He worked for a farmer for forty-five years. He had a hard life, just like all the workmen of his time. He didn't get old; the poor man never experienced the better times."

He got up and took some papers off his desk.

He could swear that the brown-covered folder was the same one the mayor had in front of him this morning.

The man sat down and lay the open dossier on his lap. He said: "And do you know what grieves me the most about my father? That he never understood it. Till his last day he gave all he had for the SDLP. He was a fanatical party member. He believed everything the party leaders told him. He never knew how he got screwed."

He got up to reach for the telephone on the desk, which had already rung twice, and listened. He said: "Let me check."

He paged through other papers lying on the desk. Then he said: "No, just send those on to Mayer."

He sat down again and took the folder from the table.

"Where were we?"

He crossed his legs and started looking through the file.

"Oh yes, my father, a fanatical socialist. Were you brought up like that too?"

He considered how he should respond. He was

thrown off a little because he was used to different treatment. They would usually start right in on him. Once in a while there would be one who would start with a friendly conversation, but they would never allow him to sit down.

He said: "I never belonged to a party."

"That's sensible, but you've been pretty active nevertheless, though it may not be in politics. I didn't read the reports all that carefully, to be honest, but when I look at . . ."

He began to scan the pages. "For example, you don't get fourteen months for nothing. That's not for riding your bike without lights. And then there's one for three months, one for four weeks, and a whole row of shorter sentences."

He should have known. At every opportunity he was reminded of his sins, and the longer the list, the heavier the punishment. That criminal record would haunt him his whole life.

"That was in another time," he said, "but for the last five years I've stayed out of trouble, as you can tell from those papers."

The man dismissed it with a wave of his hand. "Of course, I understand. If I had lived in that time, I likely would have done the same. So much injustice demands resistance. I can't stand injustice, I've always been that way."

He didn't quite know what to make of it.

"Are you a church member?"

He read in the dossier again. "I believe not, right? Of course not."

"I am nothing," he said.

"You come from a fairly anarchistic background."

He shrugged his shoulders. "I often heard my dad talk about Domela, that's true."

"The great Domela Nieuwenhuis, of course. Did you know him?"

"No, but when I was a little boy he would often come to Beets and Terwispel, and he is supposed to have been in our home too. They were proud of Domela in Beets."

"Did your family always live in that area?"

"I think so. They would move sometimes, from Terwispel to Beets, when all the peat had been dug up there. But Grampa came from Giethoorn, I've heard; a lot of folk in Beets came from there, you could tell that from their dialect. When the peat was gone in Overijsel, they came this way. They knew only how to make turf, so they had to go where the work was."

"And all of them Domela followers, of course."

"I suppose so, at least in my time. But I believe that quite a few of them first belonged to the Mennonite Church."

He said what he knew and that wasn't much. They rarely talked about it at home. Besides, he wanted to be cautious, for he didn't yet know what the man was up to. It was probably just a warm-up.

The man questioned him more closely, and then he told the story he had often heard his dad tell. That Grampa one day walked away from the meal table because he refused to read from the Bible.

"Did he have to be the one to read?"

"He was the only one who could read a little. A schoolteacher who took an interest in him must have taught him. But I think that teacher must have taught him something else as well."

The old man liked to talk big. He didn't believe that

46

it had actually happened this way, but according to Dad, Grampa must have said: The hell with it, and if that book appears on this table one more time, I will leave.

"His folks didn't want to give it up, of course."

"No, so he never came home again."

The telephone rang again and the man talked for quite a while.

He looked at the slate-blue sky. He was getting warm and he loosened the top button of his shirt. It was uncomfortable sitting in that low chair. He sank too deeply into it and he didn't know what to do with his legs.

"Give me a quarter of an hour and I'll be through with him," said the man, and hung up. He stayed behind the desk, picked up a pencil, and softly tapped the desk with it.

He said: "I'm trying to figure out what kind of a man you are. You are not a terrorist; you are too sensible for that. You have seen too much and experienced too much to let yourself be egged on by that clique in London, the so-called government in exile that never moved a finger on your behalf. Now they need you, but you know better. Am I right?"

"I have nothing to do with anything."

"I'd like to believe that. But it's possible that you don't do anything to obstruct the underground either, do you?"

The man came from behind his desk and continued: "When you are on the lake fishing and airplanes fly over and drop weapons, then you look the other way."

He noticed that the man's tone had changed and that he was looking at his watch.

"It never caught my attention."

"No, I suppose not, but if you should happen to see it, what would you do?"

He would rather have sat on a higher chair. He felt himself powerless with his legs folded almost double.

"Well, what do you say?"

"I've never witnessed that, so it is hard for me to say what I would do."

"You're avoiding the question." He looked at his watch again. "I don't have much time. You're not as innocent as I first thought. I regret that, for your sake. It doesn't make any difference to me, of course; it's a small trick to get people to confess. If we chose, you would tell us everything within an hour. But I prefer not to take that route, and I thought that with you it wouldn't be necessary either."

"I don't know what you want me to confess," he answered. "I already told the mayor this morning. I was home the whole night."

The man bounced up. "How do you know that it was this past night?"

"I gathered that. The mayor said it himself, and there were more in attendance: the water police and an officer and a regular policeman.

"I warn you that this won't do you any good. Wait, let me make it easy for you. I will tell you how it went, and you need to do nothing else but confirm the story. Shall we do it that way?"

An answer was expected of him. He said: "I didn't notice anything, so I can't say yes or no."

"Your son told us."

It came as a shock. He was going to get up, but he couldn't manage from that low chair. He managed to control himself, but uneasiness followed. He looked at the man, who kept a close eye on him, and then at the desk. He said nothing. He knew that the interrogation would now go the way he was used to, and that he would have to watch his words. It was worse now than before, because now the boy was involved. He felt himself begin to tremble inside when he thought about the boy. It started with a shiver that ran across his skin. He was scared.

"He told us everything," said the man after a short silence. "He's a lot like you. He reacted the same way. I told him the same thing. I wanted to help him because I don't believe he's bad. He was talked into it, of course, we see that happen more often. I am prepared to go easy on him. But he refused at first, so I had to send him on. I felt sorry for him when he came back in here again and confessed everything. I warned him too, just like I'm warning you now. He . . ."

"What did you do with him?"

It was the first time he had interrupted the man.

"We made him confess; just how that's done you will find out yourself if you refuse to cooperate. No one ever came away from here who ultimately didn't tell us the truth. There's nobody too tough for us to break."

He began to remember now the stories he had heard from the people in hiding. Cor, the one from Amsterdam, knew all about it, he said. And the girl knew the same kind of stories. But all of them had it secondhand. There were so many stories floating around about the Germans. He felt the rise of dread and uncertainty, and he saw the demons that had tormented him when the boy was still small. He heard him squeak and gasp in the cupboard bed next to them when the boy suffered from chest congestion, and he saw the boy's fear on his first day of school.

For fifteen years he had worried about the boy; then he turned the corner and was able to take care of himself pretty well. But at this moment the anxiety returned and slashed through his chest.

The man must be able to tell by looking at him. He said, "I want to help both of you, and there's a lot I can do for you, but then you have to help us. We've got to take care of that underground business in your area. I want the names of the leaders and then you have my word that you will be home again tonight."

"My boy too?"

"Your son too."

There was a knock on the door and the man looked at his watch. He hurried to the door and talked with somebody in the hall. When he closed the door behind him again, he said: "I don't have any more time. There are other people I can probably still help."

He sat down behind the desk and picked up a pencil. "Shall we?"

"What did you want to know?"

"I want to know everything."

"But you already know everything."

He said it innocently and he had wanted to add something, but the man didn't give him the chance. He jumped up and shouted: "This has gone on long enough. I'm not going to waste any more time on you. Confess, and at once."

But he was not that far yet. He felt himself grow more composed and then his irritability returned, too.

The man banged the table with his fist and screamed: "I'll get it out of you all right and then the whole lot of you will be lined up against the wall. And we're going to burn down that terrorist nest of yours with everything in it. We've cleaned up more of those resistance dens."

He began to breathe easier when he saw the man raging that way. He should have known; they always tried and it had never affected him. The reason that he had gotten off the track a bit this time was only because of the boy. But they didn't have him; he was certain that they hadn't caught Germ. He said: "Did he confess everything, about those resistance dens and all that?"

He felt the impulse to laugh, which had always infuriated the police.

The man was going to come at him, but he restrained himself. With large strides he rushed to the door and tore it open.

"Get this one out of here," he hollered.

A German soldier took him through the corridor in the opposite direction of the entrance, down a small concrete stairway and then through a narrow hallway with small barred ceiling lights. The soldier opened a door and gestured for him to enter. He stood in a cell and saw that he was not alone.

"Well, I'm getting company. That's nice. I've been here all by myself for days already."

It was a man in a brown corduroy suit. The elbows and the knees of the suit were shiny and the area around the fly was greasy. The man's face was wrinkled and his hair was short and gray.

He asked: "Do they keep them long here?"

Then he heard what he had been afraid of all along. The man said: "Whoever gets in here may never get out."

4.
Braaksma

If that pious schoolteacher, Braaksma, the man with the orange ribbon under the lapel, had his way, then the man in the fancy room would be on the right track now. The teacher used different words, but it amounted to the same thing. He had appeared in their yard in the fall of the first year of the war.

"A nice place," he said after he had snooped around a bit.

He was after a meal of fish, of course, but there was a fisherman in the village too, one of his own kind even.

But he knew what the man was after. A few weeks later the teacher was back again.

"Really ideal. No one is able to sneak up on you here."

But he made another trip before he came with the request: Would he be willing to give a hand now and then on behalf of the cause? He refused on the spot, and Gryt, who was there with them, said that they didn't want to get into hot water again. That irritated him, and he walked to the boat. The schoolteacher tried it out on Gryt first, and when she went inside, he came to him. He had gotten into the boat and was clawing around in the fish traps.

"But if we get somebody now and again who has to lie low for a while?"

"How do you mean that?"

"Well, there are people whose lives are in danger. If they're caught, they'll be shot."

"Anybody in trouble like that can come, but nobody else," he said.

That was good enough for the schoolteacher. Gryt was angry and she tried to talk him out of it. When that didn't work, there followed the same accusations he had listened to for years, and then came the silent treatment, which he had also become hardened to.

The first one came fairly quickly, and when he told Gryt that the man should have his food and drink on time, Gryt did not protest. They never had more than four at one time, and when the teacher tried to get him involved in other things as well, he made it very clear that he wanted no part of it. He had never had a weapon in his yard. He didn't even have his own shotgun, his father's muzzle-loader, at home.

The man in the fancy room had revealed his hand. All they had was his criminal record, and that wasn't enough to hold him. They suspected, of course, that he was involved in resistance, but they had no proof. They were just bluffing.

People in danger—he took only those. He never asked them why they needed to hide. That made absolutely no difference to him.

That had been true in '40 also, when two young men had made their home in his shed for a couple of weeks. He wasn't even sure whether one of them was Thomas' son. One evening in the first part of May they had suddenly stood in the yard, two young men in military uniform. The smaller one called him uncle and told him that he was one of Thomas's boys, and they said they'd be damned if they'd fight for queen and fatherland. He agreed with them.

Gryt was of course opposed to sheltering the boys, but he said what he would say again later: Anybody in trouble can come.

The Germans were well in control when the two boys took off again. He never heard from them again, and that was fine as far as he was concerned. He dug up the uniforms that they had buried under the shed, and Gryt made clothes for Germ out of them. He himself had gotten a lot of use from a long, green coat when he went poaching. Among the young reeds he could hardly be spotted in that coat, and, besides, the thing was almost waterproof.

"This is the first time we got something out of it," he said in jest.

But Gryt maintained that he should have sent them away.

"You should have sent them to Hindrik, he's always had a big mouth."

But Hindrik lived in a populated area, and it wouldn't have been safe there. He wanted Gryt to understand that, but it made no impression on her.

It had been different with the girl. It didn't exactly please him either that Germ had come home with her, just like that. Gryt objected even more strenuously than usual. It was the first time he felt sorry for her. She couldn't help it; that was simply the way she was.

"That girl is going to be the death of us," she said, "or of Germ."

And days later she was still complaining. This was the limit, a woman in the house who's a total stranger and then one of that kind to boot.

The straitlaced schoolteacher said: "I don't know, I don't know . . . . The Jews must be helped, of course, but whether this is the right place for such a girl . . ."

"Germ and her get along fine," he said, and then added intentionally: "They sleep together, so we don't even need an extra bed, and that helps with Gryt's washload too."

He pursued the topic, and Gryt said later: "You're just like Hindrik, he always talks dirty too."

That's where he got it, all right. Hindrik would always push it too far and turn people off.

Later the schoolteacher discussed the subject with the girl herself. It wasn't a proper thing for her to do. When he heard that, he told the teacher that he didn't want to see him in the yard again. He'd better get his fish somewhere else in the future. The schoolteacher did not come again. When he had a message, he sent someone in his place.

Maybe they were keeping his place under close surveillance today. It made no difference. Willem and Cor would take care of the girl. Willem, especially, was very much at home on the lake. Right at this moment they might be sitting in the shelter by Lolke. And Germ he didn't have to worry about at all. He must've known for some time already that something was amiss. He did hope, though, that the boy hadn't gotten too deeply involved in resistance work.

He sat on the bunk and listened with half an ear to the man, who was talking a blue streak.

The cell was cleaner than the one in Crackstate, the house of correction in Heerenveen, and the barrel didn't stink so badly either. But there were no windows. There was a ventilation shaft in the ceiling with a bit of light shining through. And a weak lightbulb shone above the door, but it was half-dark in the corners of the cell.

He sat down on the bench by the wall, right by the door. They had let him keep everything, even his chewing tobacco. He took off his jacket and hung it on the hook of his bunk. He was going to go to the barrel to take a leak when the other man suddenly jumped up.

"Just a minute, let's do it together. That lid has to stay

on as much as possible, otherwise the stink is gonna kill us. I had the runs a few days ago from the watery chow here.

"They usually empty the barrel every three days. I think they forgot me the last time, so now it stinks like the plague."

They each stood on a side, so that the lid didn't have to be off too long.

"Isn't this obscene," said the man. "But the funny thing is that for days now I haven't been able to go. From one extreme to the other. My stomach is killing me. And I can't stand this smell."

He thought that it wasn't too bad.

He sat down on the bench again and took a wad of tobacco.

"Damn, you have tobacco?"

He offered the man his pouch.

"If I only had some paper now."

He got up and in his jacket found some paper from Boonstra, the eel buyer. "Will this do?"

"Anything will do, just so it smokes. Do you have matches too?"

"That I can't help you with."

"Too bad."

The man sniffed the pouch and pulled out a pinch of tobacco. "It smells well-seasoned; this isn't homegrown. Are you in here for black market dealing too? That's what they picked me up for, see. Just some small-time stuff. You've got to make ends meet somehow, ain't that right? Everybody's got to take care of himself. It's just a case of bad luck. They could just as well have picked up the whole population."

He sniffed the pouch again and licked the tobacco he

held between thumb and index finger. "I never chewed. Does it taste good?"

He put a couple of strands in his mouth and started sucking. "Kinda strong, but I can't say it tastes bad."

He took the small wad out of his mouth and scrutinized it carefully. "Kinda dirty business, really."

"Start out easy," he said, "and don't chew too hard."

"This is real tobacco, I'd say. You can't buy this anymore."

"I trade a half pound now and again."

"Then you've gotta have pretty good stuff to trade with."

"Fish."

"Fish? Now that you mention it, you have the smell in your clothes. So you're a fish dealer."

"I fish myself, and last night I caught quite a bunch of eel. That's what you probably smell, the slime of the eel."

"Strange, though, that they let you keep the tobacco," said the man, who had sat down on the bunk.

"I still have everything."

"They forgot, of course, but that's unusual for a German. They're pretty particular, and when they goof, it's trouble. That soldier will get an immediate transfer to the front line. I've heard some strong stories about that."

The man talked too much.

"That bench is too narrow, it's hard on your back. It's more comfortable on the bunk. I speak from experience, because I've had a lotta time to try it out. I'll be here three weeks soon. I'm fed up to here with it, and I don't even know yet where I stand. First they told me that I'd be sent to the camp in Amersfoort, but that was impossible, of course. They can't put you in a camp for a little thing like that, right? They thought, of course, that I was doing the black market for people in hiding. I was interrogated for days, and that could get pretty rough sometimes. They hit me once, but an officer who was present put the kibosh on that."

The man had put the wad in his mouth and was quiet for a little while. He sucked on the tobacco while pacing back and forth. He said, "You're sitting there pretty calm, I'd say. As if you were sitting at home."

"Do they give you something to do here?" he wanted to know. "Pass the time with something or other, like gluing bags or something?"

"Something to do, work, you mean? Of course not. What would we do? I sit here the whole day with my hands folded. We can't even go outside for some fresh air, and that's pretty routine in all the jails. But this ain't an ordinary jail, of course. This is where you get interrogated. They're not equipped for outside privileges and so on. Every two days we're allowed to get out to wash ourselves. There's a little room right above here with a couple of faucets. We go in threes, but we're not allowed to talk. Did you want something to do?"

"That's what I'm used to. We always glued bags or made clothespins."

The man thought that was a good joke, he said, and wanted to know more about it. But he didn't want to pursue it anymore, because it was no joke and the man apparently didn't understand that.

He was tired; he'd like to rest a while. He inspected the upper bunk. There was no covering, but he folded his jacket double and put that under his head.

"Tonight at nine they'll bring a blanket. No mattress, nothing but a blanket. I sure had to get used to those boards at first. I'm used to sleeping on my side, but that's impossible now; your shoulder would be in pieces in the morning."

He lay down on his back and looked into the shaft, which let in a bit of fresh air and a glimmer of light.

"So you're a fisherman," the man tried again. "Where do you live, if I may ask?"

"On the northeast side of the Tjeuke Lake."

"Oh, I don't know that area. Pretty good fishing there? Of course there's a good market in fish nowadays."

It seemed like a long time ago that they had arrested him, and yet it was only half a day.

"When do we eat?" he asked.

"It's almost time, but we're not going to get fried eel, if that's what you mean."

If Boonstra had not come by this time, the line eel would probably be dead now. It didn't matter much to him anymore. Maybe the guys were cleaning now and Germ was lighting the fire under the smoke barrel. Or maybe Gryt had taken the whole business to Boonstra. In such things, she was plenty helpful. He doubted, though, that their main concern at this moment would be a bunch of fish.

"I used to love to fish," said the other. "With a pole, of course.

"But since my marriage I don't get around to it anymore. Too bad, because it can be so nice out in the fields, especially in late summer. How is the weather now? I haven't seen the sun in days."

"It's nice weather every day, still and sunny, and at night there's a dew. But the evenings are getting colder and the nights are getting longer too."

"I suppose so. And here I sit wasting my time. It

burns me up sometimes, can you believe that? Anyway, it can't be too long anymore, I hope. I haven't been summoned before the gentlemen in the last four days, and that's a good sign, don't you think?"

And then the man started jabbering again, but he didn't ask questions anymore, so he could stretch out in peace now. His body succumbed and he fell half asleep. He heard the man say that he sometimes didn't sleep a wink all night and that he couldn't understand how he could just lie down and go to sleep. He thought back to the fourteen months when during the first weeks he slept so badly too and climbed the walls at night because he thought he was losing his mind.

The door opened and the man below him sat up.

He didn't open his eyes. No one said anything. The man below him went to the door, and then he was alone. Now that he was rid of the babbling, he fell asleep, but he kept waking up with a feeling of anxiety. He wondered how it was with the boy, and the girl preyed on his mind too.

The man woke him up. "They interrogated me again. It didn't amount to anything. I think they'll let me go soon."

He was going to launch into another spiel, but a soldier entered with two plates of chow and a small can of water. The other smelled what was on the plate. "Turnips, of course, and without salt again, I bet."

He tasted it. "Just as I thought, not a grain of salt. It's strange, but I never realized how important salt is to the taste. This is no food. The first few days I seldom touched it, but I won't let that happen anymore. Two slices of bread in the morning and a mug of water, a plate of mashed potatoes and turnips at noon, and in the evening two more slices of bread—that's not enough. I must've lost ten pounds, the clothes are hanging loose on my body."

He started to eat. There was no taste to it, but he ate the plate clean.

"Maybe you're not used to much."

"That's true, though it's been getting better the last few years."

"But this is no food. I swallow it, but otherwise . . ."

"If it doesn't get worse . . ."

He meant that. As boys they often went to bed in the wintertime with a piece of turnip. Sometimes the turnips were frozen and smelled bad. A dish of potatoes with a quarter of a salted herring was a banquet.

"Maybe you can take it all right. I don't know how long you were in, but even if they locked me up for twenty years, I don't think I'd get used to it. I think I'd die inside a year."

"It's not that bad, but you don't easily get used to it, that's true."

He put the empty plate on the bench and lay down again.

"Don't you want a couple of swallows of cold water?"

He felt no need of it.

"Of course, there's enough water in what you just ate."

He took a wad of tobacco and noticed that there wasn't much left.

"I asked them how long they were going to hold me, but they didn't give me an answer. I do think, though, that I'll soon be out now. Last week they still talked about Amersfoort; they threatened me with that all the time. I found out from the detective that they paid my wife a visit and they tried to get information from the police and mayor too. They know now that I'm not a big operator on the black market and that I have nothing to do with the underground. Well, then they have to let you go, right? They also asked me what I thought of you. I said: I've hardly known the man an hour, so I can hardly tell you much about him. But when I left, he was sleeping. They found that interesting, I think. I added that you were pretty calm. I said: If you ask me, that man is wondering what he's doing here, just like me. The guilty don't sit still. Anybody who goes to sleep that peacefully can't have much to hide. Ain't that so? Or are you sleeping again?"

"No, but I can just as well be lying down."

The man sat down below him again. "Where are you from again, Tjeuke Lake, right?"

"Mailing address Delfstrahuizen."

"I think, I've been there after all. I'm from Sneek myself, that is, I've lived there since I got married. For business reasons; I deal in sheep. Sometimes I buy a cow, but I prefer sheep. Cows are hard to handle, and they take so much work. You can chase a flock of sheep into the field and they'll take care of themselves. Are there sheep in your area?"

"I've never thought about it, but I don't think so."

"I would have thought that people like you who live out in the country always have some animals, even if it's just a goat. Every day a couple of liters of rich milk and in springtime a couple of lambs. That way you can make ends meet pretty well, right?"

"I don't care much for animals."

"As a fisherman you can get along fine, of course. I'll

stop by sometime for a meal's worth of eel. As soon as I'm free I want to take a look around in your area."

"You do that."

"If they let you go soon, anyway."

"Did they ask you any more about me?"

"No, as I said, what could I tell them about you. What did they get you for, really?"

"I don't know that myself."

"Oh, that's odd. They usually don't pick you up for nothing."

"But they picked you up too, right?"

"Well yes, but I'm not entirely clean. As I said, some small-time stuff, but they thought there was more behind it."

"They must think that of me too, then."

"But there's got to be a reason for that, I'd say. Sold the fish for too much or something and . . . oh, of course, you live out in the country, right? Hiding people, maybe?"

He gave no answer.

"You've got to be careful with that. I don't want to say anything about the good ones, but you never know ahead of time what you're gonna get. There are all kinds. A brother-in-law of mine, who's a small farmer, had a couple of those Hollanders. Every night out on the road, but they never explained what they were up to. Till one night suddenly a raid, Germans all over the place, and everything turned upside down. Fortunately, they didn't find anything, but that's when I told him: You've gotta show them the door, because you're gonna pay for it otherwise. So that's what he did. I don't know your situation, but I wouldn't feel too sorry for those guys. They can take care of themselves. And those Germans here, they're not gonna let anybody screw them. All they do is interrogate people, they're experts at it. You can be as stubborn as you want, but they're gonna find you out sooner or later. I always said to myself: Never confess anything, but I've changed my mind about that. They had me trapped in no time; I was stuck in all directions, and I'm a pretty good talker usually, if I say so myself. Well, then, I simply told them the honest truth. I said: If you please, here is my story. I butchered a sheep, my wife filled all the canning jars, and for some six days or so we ate mutton. The rest went out the door and that became a treat for some others. That's all. I didn't ask where it was gonna go, that's none of my business . . . . If I had known that it was intended for people in hiding and for the underground, then they wouldn't have gotten anything from me. Because I don't want no damn trouble. We all have enough trouble of our own these days. That's exactly what I said. Do you have a family too?"

"A wife and a son."

"How old is the boy, if I may ask?"

"Twenty-one."

"A dangerous age. Did they catch him or wasn't he home?"

"I don't know where he is. They say that they have him."

"Hell, that's not so good. That's gonna be Germany for him, in a factory. Was he in the underground? Of course he was, boys like him get a kick out of that. Is he here in Leeuwarden or somewhere else?

"I don't know, but I don't think he's here."

"Was he home when they picked you up?"

"I don't know."

"If I were you, I'd meet these men halfway. Your family is at stake, right? And your own count more than strangers. Something would be wrong if it was different. All of us have the duty to stand up for our family."

He realized at once where the man was heading. He had heard this kind of talk before. As a boy already, when in the night, in Terwispel, they had beaten up the peat boss who needed straightening out.

"Remember your mother, boy." That was the village policeman, Dykstra, who tried to get him to name his buddies. "Remember your mother, she's got such a heavy cross to bear already. All the blame is going to turn on you, and that's going to hit you pretty hard." And later came the others, as reasonable as could be. First they told him that he was right; the peat boss had messed up. And they wanted so badly to do everything kindly, especially the chairman from the polder company.

"You're in a bad spot, and something has to be done about it." He asked the man right away who had sent him, and the chairman said that he shouldn't be so silly—he was acting out of the goodness of his heart.

This morning, in the fancy room, he experienced it again. They still went at it the same way.

The man below him kept on babbling. What had they promised him if he succeeded?

When they had been excluded from the government work program after the strike in '20, they had used Jan Welles for the same purpose. This has got to stop, said Jan. I've got to have work, I don't dare come home. I can't let Aeltsje and the kids starve to death. And they're willing to do right by us. If we sign the paper that we won't strike again, then we'll be back to work tomorrow.

Hindrik got mad and said: Jan Welles, if you set one foot in this house again, I'll break both your legs.

Had he been in agreement with Jan Welles then?

He said nothing now. He let the man talk, he gave no further answers. When the other man stood up, he kept his eyes closed. A bit later he heard him by the barrel. He pulled down his pants and sat down. He groaned: "I'm plugged up, it won't come. It's gonna give me trouble. That rotten food is gonna do me in yet."

He pulled his pants back up and sat down on the bench and complained of a stomachache.

He turned on his side, because his back began to hurt. "Are you sleeping again?" asked the man.

He said: "Don't bother to ask anymore, because I have nothing to say to you. And if I have to, I can take care of myself."

Then the man was silent.

5.
The Girl

Gryt said more than once that it was going to come to a bad end. The word is going to get around, she said, that we have a Jewish girl on the place. And then we'll be right back in the soup, she added bitterly.

Since this morning she must've been saying that she was right. But he was sure it wasn't the girl's fault. They hadn't come for her or for anybody in hiding. It was true that, since the girl had come, Germ was gone more often, but that was because of his trips to De Lemmer where her parents were in hiding. They were cooped up in a loft, in a small space behind a false wall. Germ had to take food over there regularly because they weren't fed enough, though they were charged plenty for room and board.

Germ had also participated in transporting weapons and in a hold-up of a ration card distribution center. Gryt did not know that and it was best that way. She already had trouble sleeping whenever she knew that Germ wasn't home.

Weeks later he heard the girl tell about that distribution center raid. She made a slip of the tongue, for Germ apparently hadn't wanted his dad to know about it either.

Later that evening when they stood together in the yard, he said to her: "I don't want Germ to get involved in everything. Tell him that. Tell him to be careful."

"Do I have to tell him that?" she had asked in surprise.

She had been with them a number of weeks already and he still did not know how Germ happened to have come in contact with her.

The prudish schoolteacher bothered himself about it too. "This cannot really be allowed. If everybody starts moving around on their own accord, the whole business is going to turn into chaos. Your son just picked up that girl. He should've consulted the organization. Or did you give him permission to take her home with him?"

The talk irritated him. He said: "No, that's not necessary here."

"Your son may do what he wants, I take it."

"Right."

"So he just came home with her one night."

"It was at dusk. They just loomed up from behind the reeds in the scow, each pulling an oar, nice as can be."

That's exactly what had happened. It had been a very quiet summer evening. They could hear the jays on the other side of the lake. He had not heard the scow come, that's how quietly they moved. Germ could punt without making any noise. When they were poaching he could even fool the ducks. He snuck up on them so quietly that he could often down two and sometimes even three in one shot.

He had been out with Kuiken that day, a fisherman from the Follegeast side of the lake. Together they could set out so many trammel nets that they could shut off whole areas of the lake. That day they caught several hundred pounds of pike and perch. He remembered it well because among the fish had been quite a few pike-perch, which he hardly ever caught on his side of the lake.

He had sat down to relax on top of the cistern that night, and Gryt joined him with a few nets that had to be mended. She was better at knitting and mending nets than he was. One of the men in hiding lay in the grass next to the shed. He had just said to Willem that it was so hard to get cotton for a new trap. Germ must have heard that. He groped behind the mast bench and held up a couple of skeins of silk.

"Will silk be okay, boss?"

He knew of course that silk would be a lot better than the coarse cotton. But silk was hard to get anywhere.

"Where did you get that, Germ?"

And then, strangely enough, he noticed the girl for the first time. She got up after Germ had pulled the bow of the scow on shore. She didn't trust herself much in that worn-out old boat.

Germ said: "There's always stuff available in De Lemmer."

They inspected the silk and agreed that it was of prewar quality. He estimated that there was enough for two traps, a nice job for Gryt.

"This is worth a fortune, old man. You can give me fifty pounds of fish to take along tomorrow."

It was worth it to him.

Germ said he knew a man in De Lemmer who took the fish to Amsterdam and sold it there for a huge profit on the black market.

Then Germ announced that he had brought a guest along, and he pointed to the girl who stood next to the scow on the grass, looking around self-consciously. Germ motioned for her to come. She came shyly to him and shook his hand. Gryt put down the fish trap and stood up. The girl shook her hand too and said that her name was Mirjam. Germ asked Gryt where she could sleep.

"What's going on, Germ?" Gryt wanted to know.

"Well, nothing special. She wasn't allowed outside anymore in De Lemmer, and it's not easy always to be cooped up, right?"

"In De Lemmer they have Feldgendarmerie and those scoundrels are dangerous," said Willem. "They patrol the roads day and night and stop everybody."

He told Gryt to warm up the coffee and he himself hauled the cane chair out of the house. While he was carrying that through the hallway, Gryt, who was standing by the kerosene burner, said: "This is going to be trouble. You've got to speak up now."

He set the chair next to the cistern and asked the girl to sit down. Germ had sat down on the far end of the cistern and was talking to Willem. The boy paid no attention to the girl. He was of course a bit embarrassed about it; he had never brought a girl home before. Gryt and he didn't even know that he had a girlfriend.

He noticed that the girl felt very uncomfortable. He said to her: "Why don't you help me a minute; I want to wind this up into a ball." He put a skein across her hands, and he told Germ to get a jacket because the girl was shivering in the evening air.

The girl said: "I'm not cold, but it is so quiet here and there's so much space."

Willem said that she'd get used to that just like he had. He said: "It's a quiet evening. It's not often this way."

Germ explained to the girl that in the wintertime the water would often get up to the threshold of the house and that last winter they had to build a sod embankment to hold the water back.

The girl stared across the meadows where a few cows were grazing in the upcoming dew. And then at the mist that was coming up out of the lake, slowly creeping closer.

He himself had never quite got used to it either. There was too much water and too much grass here. He liked the peat puddles with hedgerows of alders and willows between.

The haze from the lake always brought with it the

smell of manure and cow sweat that he couldn't stand. He preferred the musty smell of peat and mud.

"Here's some coffee," Gryt said stiffly.

She put the cups on the cistern and took her chair inside.

He gave the girl one of the cups. "Drink it while it's still warm."

Her long fingers trembled a little and sometimes her mouth quivered.

She was a good-looking girl, a bit dark-skinned, with sharp facial features.

She looked at Germ, who had his back toward her and was talking to Willem.

He said: "If you like lots of space, you'll not be disappointed here. You're free to roam where you want, but don't get too close to the road. When you see the police boat heading this way, get lost for a while. The officer has a pair of binoculars and he loves to aim it our way. Don't worry too much about anything else. The grocer has his regular times and Boonstra, the eel merchant, comes only when we ask him to. And Gryt knows the day the bakery man comes. You'll get used to the routine."

The girl said: "It'll take me a while to get used to it. There's so much space here."

"A nervous wreck," Gryt said later.

6.
The File

The man in the fancy room was not alone at first. An officer sat next to him, a high-ranking one, from all appearances, but he soon left. The soldier, however, had taken up his post at the door.

First he had to stand and wait while the man remained seated behind the desk. The man took his time, studying the reports and papers and taking notes. He pretended not to notice that someone stood before his desk.

At last he put his pencil down and looked up.

He said: "I got too carried away this morning. I've been too busy and that gives me a short fuse. But you weren't being very sensible, either. Now I've read your whole file, and I also got a report on what happened at the lake early this morning. I have a better perspective now."

He put his hand on the papers inside the brown cover.

"I've already told you that I understand your kind of people. My father was also a laborer. Wait, let's sit down."

He had to sit in that low chair again in which he preferred not to sit, and the man took his seat across from him.

"Please tell me the story of those fourteen months now. Of course, I have the official reports. I know the facts and according to the record, you had it coming. It's an airtight case. But the reports don't tell everything, sometimes not even the truth. The reality is different; the reports lie."

The man crossed his legs. His shoes were still just as shiny as this morning. He straightened the crease in his pants and took a cigarette out of a wooden box.

"Tell me how things really went."

He hesitated. "It's so long ago, and if you already know about it . . ."

"No, you don't understand. I want to hear it from you."

He thought for a moment. "It must have been during that severe winter of '22. I remember it because I was just married then."

"In '22, that's right. You were born in 1894, so you were twenty-eight then. You were not exactly in a hurry."

The man picked up the brown folder and paged through it.

"I didn't have a steady job, and I didn't want to get married all that bad either."

"Often unemployed, of course."

"Yes, that's the way it often was at that time, and employers weren't all that crazy about us either."

"On account of your political activities."

"We didn't care about politics, we just cared about getting a few cents more per hour."

"But when a strike was called, you'd be in the front row."

"Not me so much, Dad and my brothers were more fanatical."

"Your son was born in '22, I notice. Let me see, that wasn't a voluntary wedding, I'd say."

"No, we had to get married, otherwise I wouldn't have done it. I had no money and I was often in Germany."

"Yes, I want to come back to that pretty soon. But first your story about those fourteen months."

"That was in Duurswoude. We poached a lot to make ends meet. We would get two quarters in Gorredijk for a wild rabbit and a guilder for a full-grown hare. For a

82

deer we'd get more than a week's pay. But it wasn't easy to catch a deer, and then you'd have to take it to a game shop at night, otherwise it wasn't safe. In Duurswoude I got a game warden after me, and so I took a shot at him."

"That was at least attempted homicide. You got off easy with fourteen months for that. I assume you know that as well. Poaching is a violation, but to shoot at an innocent game warden is a serious offense. And yet you did it. Why did you shoot at that man?"

"We were in a bind. My wife became bedridden with the pregnancy and things didn't look good. I couldn't leave. Otherwise I would've let myself get caught, because as a bachelor I'd been jailed more often and I didn't mind that so much. Especially not in wintertime, because then they would have one less to feed at home."

"But they caught you anyway."

"He started bellowing like a bull, and he didn't get up. That hadn't been my intention. I just wanted to nick him so he wouldn't pursue me anymore. But I had an old gun, it wasn't too accurate, and you'd never know exactly where the buckshot would hit. I was scared that I had hit him in the face, and when he didn't get up and started to holler, I was afraid he might freeze to death. Because it was freezing hard that night."

His mouth was dry from all the talking.

"And then?"

"I took him to his home, and we came to a firm understanding that nothing would be said about this. But he didn't keep his end of the deal."

"Right, he reported you anyway."

"Maybe they forced it out of him. He was laid up with it for quite a while, and they must've asked him about all those puncture wounds. Because his body was full of buckshot. He had to see a doctor about that, of course. And that could not be kept quiet."

"He could have made up some kind of explanation."

"I told them that he snuck up on me and that I mistook him for a deer, and he told them that he wasn't sure exactly what happened. So he covered up, but I think he did that because he was scared of us."

"And you went in the slammer for fourteen months."

"That's right."

"Who took care of things at home?"

"My own family took them in. They didn't have anything either, but they could at least keep the stove heated. And Hindrik helped himself to some baskets of potatoes from a farm in Koartsweagen, and that's how they struggled through the winter."

"Stealing potatoes, you said?"

"Yes, the truck farmers had the potatoes in mounds, covered with a bunch of straw and a good layer of dirt. Then they wouldn't freeze so easily. We'd often open up a mound like that and help ourselves to some potatoes. It was quite a job sometimes when the frost was very deep. Then you'd need a hatchet and that would make a lot of racket. And the farmers would be on the alert, of course."

"And there wasn't any one in authority who gave your sick wife a second thought?"

"Of course not."

"Exactly; and now those seven months."

"How I got those? That was earlier, much earlier. I don't think I was twenty yet then. They were striking everywhere. In Beets we called it bullchasing, and every morning we had roll call on the corner by the tavern. That's where the Royal Police would come, too. They would surround us on horseback, and if things went too far for them, they would let the horses advance a few steps. After a while we would practically stand on top of each other, and that way they could keep us under control. But that time something went wrong, I'm not sure how anymore. I still remember that they knocked Strampel, the guy in charge of roll call, off the horse-feeders with a flat saber. In the horse-feeders you'd stand above the crowd for a better view."

"What was the roll call?"

"Well, we'd talk about what should be done, to hang in there and continue the strike or to give up. It depended on what the employers would pay."

"Everybody was fighting, you say, for when the Royal Police started to flail away, then you would start too."

"We defended ourselves. What else could we do? But we couldn't get anywhere close to overpowering them, of course. We took a lot of beatings."

"But that isn't what got you those seven months."

"There were four of us, and we all got the same. I can still remember that Hindrik grabbed the horse's mouth."

"Who is Hindrik?"

"The second oldest. There were six of us kids, five boys and a girl. There was another but she died young. I never knew her, and Jantsje is no longer living either. Germ and Bareld went to America, Germ first and Bareld a few years later. We've never heard anything from Bareld since."

"That Hindrik, is he still alive?"

"Yes, and Thomas too; at least I've had no news that something happened."

"What line of work are those men in?"

"What they're doing at the moment, I don't know.

Hindrik always did manual labor, and Thomas is supposed to live in Houtigehage. He did some dealing and he kept a lot of chickens."

"You don't go there much?"

"No, we don't run each other's doors down. It's years since I've been in Beets."

"You had trouble or something?"

"We've never had trouble, but they live too far out of the way and we all have our own life."

"All right, you were talking about Hindrik."

"Hindrik grabbed the horse by the mouth, I know that. As long as you had hold of the horse's bit, they weren't able to hit you so easily. You could duck under the horse's neck and at the same time kick the horse in its belly. The horse would then throw his rear end up in the air, and if you were lucky, the rider would come flying off. And otherwise he'd have all he could do to stay in the saddle instead of giving you a beating. But this one was able to hit us because there was a foal in that horse and Hindrik was an animal lover, and so he didn't want to kick the horse in the belly. I was hit on my shoulder with the dull side of the saber and that hurt like hell. The others were furious too, and together we tore him off that horse and gave him a good drumming. The whole ruckus wasn't necessary, really, because we had already agreed to go back to work."

"It wasn't necessary, you say, but the judge couldn't care less about that."

"I think we did tell him that. The police just plowed right in and started flailing away. But I don't think they wanted to listen to us."

"Exactly, that's what I want you to see. Pretty soon I won't have to explain anything anymore. Let's go a little

86

further now. How did you get . . . let's see, those four weeks. I'm just picking one of them."

He didn't remember; he had served so many of those short sentences. And the man made him suspicious. He was too decent.

"It must have been for poaching. The district judge in Beets had it in for poachers because we spent a lot of time in his woods."

The man's smile grew bigger all the time. It seemed he was having a good time. Dad had a saying that you rarely say too little when you face your interrogator. Remember, everything you tell them can be used against you. But that was about other things, of course. This was a discussion about the past and he didn't have to hide anything. Besides, it was all in that file anyway.

"And why did you poach?"

"Well, as I said, to make a living. We didn't eat the catch ourselves. We took it to the game shop dealer and with the money we'd buy American bacon and lard."

"You were so hard up that you had to poach."

"That's about the way it was, but we sorta enjoyed it too."

"Did you ever come across a judge who took into account that this was your only means of making a living? Did the judge who gave you those fourteen months have any idea that your family could not get along without you? Of course not, they never gave that a thought. A common laborer was of no account, a common laborer had no right. And now my question: Do you want those people back in power, must we have those conditions again in the future, must the time come again when the workers have no rights? What's your answer to that?"

"Not as far as I'm concerned," he said.

"That's what I would say, too. Never again, of course. That time will never come back, we'll make sure of that. But the people need to understand that it's going to take some doing. They should help us, and you too. You know what the world is like."

The man stood up and went to his desk. "Think about that for a while. If you use your good sense, ultimately you'll have to agree with me."

He began to understand that they were not yet finished. He waited for more and looked outside. The sun came from the side and lit the windows on the other side. The sky was still slate-blue. It must be hot at home, especially behind the shed.

"What do you say about that?"

The man started pacing back and forth.

"What can I say. The police who wanted to get me in the past are still after me, and I believe the mayors are still exactly the same."

"This has little to do with a few policemen and a mayor, of course. If you have any complaints about the treatment, though, then you have to say so, because that will be investigated. That has changed a great deal. But that isn't what's at stake here. This is something much bigger."

"I don't know much about it; I spend very little time with people and I have nothing to do with anybody in particular. And that's the way I like it."

"You feel let down. You had ideals but nothing turned out. Isn't that true?"

"We just wanted to get ahead a little, that's all."

"You wanted to improve your lot in life, that was your ideal."

"If you want to call it that . . . ."

"And now you think everything is futile."

"We're already doing better. The fish bring a good price."

The man stopped and looked down on him. "Why did you leave Beets really?"

"I just happened to fall into this fishing business. I didn't have a job at the time, so it was easy to give this a try."

"But you had steady work just before then."

They were well informed. They even knew about that polder incident that he preferred not to talk about.

"That was just for a little while, and it wasn't my kind of work."

The man did not pursue it and he was glad of that.

"Let us accept that you have nothing to do with people and that you really don't care so much what's going on in the world today. Let us further accept that you were home during the night and that you noticed nothing about what was happening on the lake . . . ."

"That's the absolute truth. I already said that this morning. If it happened on the other side of the lake, that could easily be because with this wind the noise drifts in the opposite direction. And I also said that we sleep in cupboard beds and you don't hear much in those."

"Good, I believe that. But you live out in the country, an ideal place for those who prefer not to associate much with other people, isn't that so?"

"That's possible, but I can't help that I happen to live there."

"You're playing dumb. I will accept that you have little to do with anything anymore. I can understand that, considering your past. But I cannot believe that nobody has ever come to you with certain requests. Or am I wrong."

"I don't understand."

"You understand me all right, but I'll say it in so many words. If I needed a place to hide, I'd come to you."

"I want nothing to do with that."

"Agreed, but did no one ever come to ask?"

"They know me. They know how I feel about that. And they're all a bunch of pious fanatics around there who don't even trust me."

"You're not answering my question."

"Like I said, they know what kind of person I am. They don't come to me. It wouldn't work, either. We have a small house with only one room. Where would we put them."

The man held up a report. "It says here that they counted four beds this morning in that small house of yours. Isn't that excessive?"

"I already explained that this morning when policeman Bolhuis asked about it. In the summertime I often sleep in the back of the house because it's not as stuffy there as in the cupboard bed, and the bed in the attic is the boy's."

He said that intentionally, and he waited to see if the man would start talking about Germ.

"You've also been to Germany, right? We were going to get back to that. Was that for a long stay?"

"Never longer than six, seven months at a time, and a whole bunch of us would go "

"You made good money there, isn't that so?"

"We were able to save some money there."

"Did you work for a farmer?"

"No, we didn't care for farmwork. And I didn't know

how to milk. I spent some time in the mines, but most of the time we worked on the railroad and road building. They were putting in a lot of new tracks and roads at that time."

"What did you think of Germany?"

"There was more work there and the people were better off there than we were here, at least at that time. But there was also a time that the Germans came here to help with the mowing and the haying and so on, you must know that too."

"Sure, but that was a different time. When you were there, national-socialism was on the rise and that helped you get work. You had Hitler to thank for being able to save some money there."

"It's true that something was going on there, but we didn't have much to do with that. We had our own group and we were there to work."

"Did you never think about staying in Germany?"

"We had our home in Beets and that's where we wanted to be. I'm not sure why."

"Some did stay there, though."

"Not from our area, but I did hear about some. That was later; I haven't been back there since 1937."

"Those people were a lot better off. I talked to a lot of Frisians in Recklinghaus who were happy to be there. They know the difference between old and new times, and that's why they also know now which side to be on. Right now much is demanded from those people. The men are on the front line, the women in the factories. Here we hardly do anything. Germany is doing everything for us. I'm not asking you to do anything either. All I need from you is some information. It makes no difference to us if you say nothing, we'll find out everything anyway. It's only a small detail to arrest several hundred people. There are always some among them who start talking right away. But we'd rather not do that. The innocent often become the victims and it creates a lot of commotion. I believe that you're a good man. And I know very well how the common people think about this; they're willing, but they don't dare. They're being terrorized by a small group of people who realize that their time is past, but they want to resist to the end because they have everything to lose. I had thought that you had more courage. And I still believe that. You are no coward; these reports make that clear enough. You have always dared to stand up for your convictions."

He lay the brown folder on his desk. He took a cigarette and lit it. He waited, but there was no response. Then he said with a sigh: "Well, we'll just leave it at this, then."

The German soldier got the signal and came forward.

He pulled himself up out of his chair and hesitated for a moment. He said: "This is a mistake. I have nothing to say. I have no part in it and I want to have nothing to do with it. That's not forbidden, is it? I have my fishing and right now I'm making a pretty good living with that. I don't need to get involved in anything else. Why do I have to be implicated in this? I don't even want to know about it, it's none of my business. Why should I give a damn what they're up to on the lake during the night. Just so they leave my fish traps alone."

He took a step toward the man. "And if you want to tell me that nowadays they no longer deliver a common worker into the hands of the big shots, then tell me how it's possible for me to be picked up just like that? They used to tell me right away what they wanted me for, but you don't even do that. You treat people whichever way you want. I have nothing to do with the whole rotten business and I'll be damned if I'm going to stay here any longer."

The soldier grabbed his shoulder.

When he walked through the corridor, his shaking stopped. He wiped his sweaty hands on his pants and let himself be locked up.

7.
The
Cigarette
Box

"How did it go?" asked the other.

He stood under the light with his hands on his back and looked him up and down.

"All right."

He lay down on the bunk.

"What do you mean, all right?"

"Or not all right, I don't know exactly."

"I was called back again too."

"That's what I thought."

"How would you know?"

"They gave you something to smoke."

"Damn."

He put his hand in front of his mouth. "You smelled that, of course. I could smoke as much as I wanted. I smoked four cigarettes in a row, enough to make me sick, but now I've had my fill of them for a while. They were pretty decent. Some of them are scoundrels of course, but there are a couple you can really talk to. You shouldn't be too hard on those people, of course. After all, they got their orders too and let me tell you, far from home in a foreign land and among people that would like to see them dead. That ain't easy. It shouldn't surprise us that they sometimes go too far. And . . ."

"What was the message?" he asked.

"What they said to me? Well . . ."

"No, what you have to say to me."

"Oh, well, yeah, they did talk about that. You were on to that this morning already. I didn't tell them everything. I'm in a bad fix, just as bad as you are, and it's worth a good deal to me if I can get outta here. I've got a family with three young kids. I can . . ."

He grabbed his stomach and doubled up. "There it is again, a cramp in my guts." He ran to the barrel and pulled his pants down. As he sat down, he groaned: "This can't go on, the whole business is plugged up. I'm gonna have to ask for a doctor."

His talking turned into moaning.

He saw that the man's pain was real. He said: "Now that you've smoked, maybe it'll come. When I smoked my first pipe as a boy, I had to go like a cow full of spring grass afterward."

The man grunted some more but said that nothing was coming.

He lay down on his back and stared into the ventilator shaft. He was gradually beginning to relax again. But he was very tired. I can't take it as well as I used to, he thought.

When he was first married, he often thought about it, sometimes every day. After the discussion about Germ and Bareld with the man in the fancy room it came back now: the feeling of regret that he hadn't gone to America. Germ had very much wanted him to because he really didn't dare go alone.

I should've done it, I should've done it. There were times he had thought that more than once every day. Everybody seemed to be going. Guys of seventeen, eighteen years old went across and reported that they were making money to burn.

He could've afforded it. The trip at that time cost eighty guilders and he'd sometimes come back from Germany with that much money. At one time they had spent a whole summer in peat work without striking once, and he could have gone after that summer.

After he got stuck with Gryt he still had it in his head. If it hadn't been for the boy, he would have gone through with it. There would've been somebody else to go along. He got along well with Jaap Dykstra and together they would've made out fine.

"You don't have to stay here for my sake," said the old man. "If I was ten years younger, I'd still try it myself."

"What prevents you?" said Hindrik. "You're still in good shape and they can use ornery types like you in America."

Hindrik did not want to go to America for all the gold in the world. When they worked in Germany he got as homesick as a cat. He didn't go as often as the others, either. They were able to make it at home. "My old lady can get along on a shoestring," he used to say.

"It won't come," sighed the other man as he put the lid back on the barrel.

"The cramp's over for right now, but it'll come back, of course."

Bent over, he stumbled to the bench and sat down.

He didn't like the man, right from the start he hadn't, but he could see that the man had a bad case. In a few minutes the man doubled over from a new attack.

"Sit down on your knees and then let yourself sag down so that you're squeezing your stomach, that will help."

The man looked at him funny. "Is that s'posed to be a joke?"

"No, just try it. As kids when our bellies were empty, we would do it too. You're pinching your guts together that way, and that gives relief."

"But my trouble ain't from hunger, but because I'm all plugged up."

"That makes no difference. It works great for a gut-ache too. It'll make you go pretty soon. A little bit of peppermint oil would work even better. If we could afford it, Mom would often have some of it in the house and then we would get half a teaspoonful. She had it in her apron pocket when we worked in the peat together. As boys we'd be treading around in the scoop and Mom would wheelbarrow the first squares into a pile. In the fall we'd have a constant cold, and then we needed her. But when she wasn't there, we'd sag through the knees and squeeze our bowels."

The man knelt on the floor and tried it.

"Make 'em pinch," he said, and he turned on his side to watch how the man did it.

After a while, the man grunted: "I'll be damned, I think it's working."

"Just stay sitting that way. According to my mom, you shouldn't do it for more than fifteen minutes, otherwise you're going to have trouble. But I don't know anymore what kind of trouble. She had a lot of those cures that cost nothing."

He suddenly remembered that he had talked about America with the girl. The subject came up when she said that in 1939 her dad wanted to emigrate, preferably to America, because they had relatives there. Dad was afraid that the Netherlands would not be able to stay neutral in the world war that was sure to come.

"He should've done it," she said.

"I should've done it too," he said.

Together they were checking up on the fish traps. It was an outing for her and she could lend a hand when necessary. He had a fish trap in hand that in all probability had had a visit from an otter, judging by the hole. He explained to her what such an animal looked like. He had put the boat on the leeward side of a clump of bulrushes and was knitting the holes in the trap. While watching his skill, she told him about her family. "We should've gone to America."

He told her then that more than once he had been ready to take off.

"And it would've been easy to do. I've got two brothers there and one would've been willing to help us. I've often been sorry that I didn't go through with it."

"Did they do well in America, those brothers of yours?"

"I think so, at least they never came back."

"You mean they never wrote about it?" the girl wanted to know.

"We never went to school much, and we didn't keep it up either, so letter writing doesn't come so easy. But Germ often sent a picture postcard with a few words that he was doing fine."

"And the other brother?"

"We never heard from him again; he didn't get along with Dad."

"Did he run away or something?"

"No, we didn't have trouble, but the morning he left he gave Dad a good beating."

He went on to tell her how Bareld had put his knapsack down, walked over to the old man and said to him: "And now you're going to get what you've got coming, because you let our mom die, you old skunk."

And that was true. Dad was rough on himself and even rougher on Mom and the kids. The big boys could take it, but mom couldn't. Bareld said that he had let her die. He rammed Dad in the chest and punched him in the stomach three times, and then he flung him into the canal. Bareld put his knapsack on his back and that's how he left.

The girl looked at him and asked cautiously: "Was your dad so terrible then, or was your brother . . ."

"Bareld was not a bad fella. He is older than me and so he lived longer with Mom. According to Hindrik, he was crazy about her."

"And what did your dad do then?"

"Nothing. He'd pretty much had his fill of it, I think. We hauled him out of the water or he would've drowned because he couldn't swim. He did stand there for quite a while looking after Bareld, but Bareld never looked back."

It was almost too much for her, he noticed.

"What did he say about your dad again?"

"He said that he had let our mom die. Mom was sick a long time, I still remember that. Our boat lay in a stream then by the Prikroad. It was mostly water then and there were almost no houses. We lived on a small flat barge on which Dad had built a cabin. I don't know what was ailing Mom, nobody paid too much attention to that, but it was likely consumption, there was a lot of that going around. We didn't get much to eat of course, and Mom even less, the kids came first. And the food wasn't the right kind. Mom needed eggs and milk and so on."

"And wasn't that available?"

"It was available all right, but we couldn't afford it. Maybe Mom could've gotten help, but then Dad would've had to go to relief for the poor in Beetsterzwaag. They would give handouts sometimes, not much of course, and usually no eggs or other expensive foods. And for Dad that would've been a hard trip to make."

"Why?"

"Dad didn't want to hold out his hand, he was too proud for that. He was sorta extreme and his reputation wasn't the best, so I don't know if they would've helped him. He was a fanatical Domela-man. Domela Nieuwenhuis was his man, whatever he said was the law for him. Domela was the leader of the anarchists and the gentlemen in Beets were not fond of those."

"He never tried to get help for your mom?"

"I don't think so."

"But if your mom was so terribly sick . . ."

"Maybe he didn't even realize that himself. They probably didn't even have a doctor out to see her. And Mom never complained."

The girl got on his nerves a bit with all those questions.

"But would you do it if your wife was terribly sick?"

He said that he didn't know.

"Germ never tells me anything about Beets and so on," said the girl.

"Germ doesn't know that much! He was still a boy when we left there."

"But you don't tell him anything, either. Why not?"

"He's never asked about it, I guess."

At another time she had remarked that Germ and he said so little to each other and that he and Gryt would be silent for a whole evening.

"And you tell me a whole lot."

He replied that talking to strangers seemed to come a bit easier.

"Should that be about enough?" asked the other man. "The pain is mostly gone."

"Why don't you try it."

"If I could get rid of something now . . ."

The man got up and grunted. "I don't even have to try it."

He went back to lie down on the bunk.

"Lay on your back and pull your knees up, up to your shoulders if you can, then it won't come back, maybe."

"How do you know all about these things?"

"As I said, at home we had to take care of ourselves, and what Mom taught us then we still profit from. We never had a doctor out to our place."

"You mentioned something about my message a while ago."

He waited. "I said, you wanted to know a while ago what message I had."

"I heard you."

There was a short silence. "They want me to pump you and then report it to them. If that works, they'll let me go."

"That's what I thought."

"I told them I was willing, but that there was no use trying to put anything over on you. Just after you left for your interrogation, I had to appear before the other man to give a report of what you had said. I tried to give them something, but those guys are sharp, I tell ya. They caught on right away that I'd found out nothing. So now you know how things stand."

He heard the squeaking of the bunk under him. The man tossed and turned and passed gas. "Well, at least that one's out."

Then came the sound of soldier boots down the hallway, but they went past.

The man said: "And then they started to threaten. They said that I had to try again or it would turn out bad for me."

"But they did let you smoke cigarettes."

"That was later, after I explained it to them."

"What did you explain to them?"

"That you weren't born yesterday, so to speak. Well, what are you gonna do. I'm up a creek and that's why I'm telling them straight out what the lay of the land is. I want to get the hell outta here. I'll go stir-crazy here before long."

"You'll get over that, of course."

"Not me, I'll go outta my mind if I stay here any longer."

"The first few weeks are the worst, that's true."

"This is no prison, this is a transit house. The people who refuse to cooperate end up here. Did you see that long corridor right around the corner here? They have rooms there for the big-timers who refuse to confess. During the night I sometimes suddenly hear somebody scream and then soldiers start running through the hall. That kinda thing always seems to be done during the night."

"Is that where you were questioned?"

"No, but that's what I'm scared of."

"So, you haven't confessed yet."

"I don't have anything to confess, that's the problem. I've told them everything I know, but that's not enough. There are a lot of people in the underground in Sneek, they said, and they thought I would be able to tell them more about that. But I know nothing. I'm a dealer and I want nothing to do with the underground. But they don't believe that."

"Yeah, that's the way it usually is."

"It's the honest truth; they think I'm mixed up in all kindsa stuff, but all I did was a little dealing. I bought a bunch of ration cards, but if I'd known they were taken from a distribution center by the underground, I wouldn't've touched them, of course. But how was I to know? I made the deal with the man in the alley next to the cafe by the public market. I can't even tell you what he looked like because it was almost dark. That's all, but they don't believe me. I told them. I said: Do you think those people of the underground are crazy? They're not about to throw in their name and address, you know. Detectives should certainly be able to understand that!"

"And now they just let you sit here."

"The first few days I had to do nothing but try to identify people they had arrested, but I didn't know any of 'em. But that gradually got less, and I started to hope that I would get off with that."

"Maybe they're still after some others they want to show you, and that's why they're still keeping you."

"I don't know, I'm all mixed up. I wish there was more I could tell those guys. If I only knew as much as you do."

"I know even less. I've never bought ration cards. I sell fish and I know exactly where they come from, because I take them out of the lake myself."

"They seem pretty sure, though, that you know a lot more."

"I get the same feeling."

The man below him sat up and held up his hand as if to seal an agreement by handsmacking. "I want to make a deal with you. Nobody's gonna find out, the Germans don't have to know about it. I'm gonna tell them that you made a slip of the tongue. I'll give you ten thousand guilders to boot. I've got a nice bunch of sheep in the fields on the other side of Sneek. We'll go there together and then we'll close the deal. My hand on it, and it stays between us. It's in the interest of both of us, right? You don't have to tell the Germans everything. If they just have a lead, they'll take care of the rest. You've gotta think about your family, nobody else will. And you don't have to do a thing yourself."

The man held up his hand again and looked at him with eager eyes.

He said: "This is a rotten business. You know a lot more about the underground than I do."

Then the man began to sob nervously and suddenly dashed to the barrel with his hands clutched to his stomach. Halfway there he dropped to his knees and squeezed his belly.

"I'm gonna die, I'm gonna die, and you too, goddamn you, we're both gonna die. Tell them something, man. Why should we give a damn about the people."

He kept whining and wailing while pinching his gut more and more and swaying his rear end back and forth.

He was still lying down when a soldier entered, looked at him, and told him to get up. The man had not noticed him and jumped up. But he immediately folded double again with his hands on his stomach, and he hollered that the pain was killing him. The soldier ignored him, stepped to the bunk and said: "Come along."

He put on his jacket and followed the soldier.

They went back to the fancy room and the soldier stopped on the doormat. The sun just touched the top of the houses on the other side. The blinds had been pulled up, and he saw people behind the windows.

"Your last chance," said the man, businesslike.

He was not offered a seat.

"I don't think you understand what that means. If we don't come to an agreement this time around, I won't be able to do anything for you anymore."

He looked at him and continued: "Now we're going to do it without the embellishments of this morning. I've tried to be decent with you, I've given you every opportunity, isn't that so?"

"I s'pose so," he said.

"I will now give you straightforward questions and I expect straightforward answers. Let's have that clearly understood. This is the first question: You have no contacts with the underground?"

"No, I said that already and . . ."

"Stop; I said without embellishments. How did your son join the underground?"

He felt the old anxiety creep up on him again. He said slowly: "I don't know if he joined. I don't believe so."

"He joined, all right. He just turned twenty-one, he's of age. But can he do all of that without your knowledge?"

"If you say that he did join, then that happened without my knowledge."

"Where was he last night?"

"That I don't know, he was not at home."

"You just let him run. You have no authority over him. That boy can do whatever he wants."

"From early on we've had to learn to take care of ourselves."

"That's how you were raised, and that's the way it is with your son, too."

"That's always been our way."

"He should have been in Germany. He was called up, but you wouldn't know about that either, of course."

"I don't remember that."

"But it's true. I had somebody look it up. He was called up for Germany."

"It's not our way to let ourselves be ordered."

The man suddenly jerked a drawer open and put a few things on top of the desk: a well-worn tobacco case, a pocketknife, and a tin cigarette lighter.

He saw it at once. He didn't even have to see it from closer up, yet he took a step forward and stared at the tobacco case, the F. Herder, and the lighter that the boy often fussed around with because it worked so poorly.

He felt himself get sick, a feeling he had not had before, and that was much worse than the shaking and the sweating.

The man behind the desk was silent.

He wanted to say something, but he couldn't think of anything. He would have liked to sit down now, even in that low chair if necessary, because his legs were shaking.

The man said: "We always have more than one trick up our sleeve."

The trembling did not subside, and the sick feeling in his stomach didn't either.

At last he said: "You've got him."

The man answered: "We've got him."

8.
Bananas

What he had said to the girl last spring, when they had checked on the fish traps together, was not altogether true. He had made that journey to the relief office. Gryt had urged him to do it for the first time when she was pregnant.

They were in a little houseboat by the Swyns Road then. He had bought it in Oudeboorn. It was a ramshackle little boat that would hardly move anymore. They had a hard time getting it through Boorn to the Beetster canal. Hindrik pulled the towline, and he himself bailed water all the way. By the Swyns Road the boat almost sank right from underneath them. When they saw an inlet they quickly pulled the boat into it. Then they shoveled a few wheelbarrows full of peat soil and threw that and a bunch of branches under it, and then they secured the four corners to posts so the boat couldn't sink any deeper. And that's how they happened to get stuck by the Swyns Road.

He didn't have a penny when they got married. Gryt had a job at a bakery in Tynje but was fired as soon as they found out she was pregnant. They didn't want her at home because there were already too many mouths to feed. So he had to take her home to his family. Since Mom's death there had not been a woman in the house. It was a mess of a place that got the best of Gryt in a hurry. Not worth a dime as a cook, his dad pronounced, you bought yourself a pig in a poke—while Gryt was sitting right there.

When she was four or five months along, Gryt had to stay in bed. He was without work just like other men in Beets, but with Hindrik and Dad as partners they managed to get along. Twice that winter they poached a deer in the Zwargiter woods, and with a couple of old trammel nets they hauled bucketfuls of fish out of the peat canals by the Stobbehoeke.

Gryt wanted to see a doctor because she was gradually getting worse, she said. Hindrik and Dad were of the opinion that it was a waste of money, and Hindrik's wife Geeske added that it was all in her head. Gryt was a whiner and a complainer, they said.

Still, he did take her in to Boorn, pulling her on a sleigh. He dressed her warmly and took Geeske along. They didn't get much help from the doctor, but he didn't charge much either.

Four weeks later came that ruckus with the forest ranger that got him the fourteen months sentence. They picked him up just before the work started, and when he got out of Crackstate the work was about to start again. The boy had come in the meantime, a sickly little kid, according to Dad and Hindrik. Gryt had visited him once at Crackstate with the little boy who cried constantly and had started to scream when he saw his dad. Don't bring him along again, he ordered Gryt.

Germ was closest to him, and so they had agreed to name the boy after Germ. Dad didn't object. There were two Lykles in the family already, and since neither one amounted to anything, there was no sense in adding any more.

After he was released from the house of correction, they worked for only about three weeks. Then a strike was called because the peat bosses wanted to reduce their pay. He couldn't really afford to be without income. Gryt wasn't able to nurse, the baby had to have sweet milk, and so forth. First he made a trip to Gryt's parents in Boornbergum, but they could barely take care of themselves. For the boy's sake he had gone to the relief office in Beetsterzwaag. He didn't tell his dad and the others about it. From the relief office he got a note that he could take to the store in Beets for some baby food, and twice a week he could get a liter of milk from a farmer in Oudbeets.

A bit later he worked now and then at some odd jobs: loading a boat in Gorredijk and unloading railcars. The pay was poor, but to earn more he'd have to go to the clay region in Groningen, and he didn't want to be that far from his boy.

For a while he had been all set to take a steady job as a farmworker in Boorn. That didn't look so bad. He didn't have to milk, and it came with a one-room brick house, including a rainwater cistern and pump. Gryt had been very excited about that. The boat was damp and moldy and very bad, especially for the boy.

But when Dad heard about it, he had been spittin' mad. And Hindrik had said: "Did you lose your marbles? One of us working for a farmer, how crazy can you get! If you don't dare do it yourself, I'll tell Gryt what's what."

He said: "I'm not doing it for Gryt's sake, but because of the boy."

Nevertheless, he did not take that job, and before he told Gryt, he had more drinks in a tavern by the bridge than he could handle, so then she didn't dare give him a hard time, for drinking always put him in an ugly mood.

And yet they pulled the boy through.

"It's the bananas," said Gryt.

Every week he went to Gorredijk to buy a kilo of bananas, and the boy would get a couple of those a day. Gryt mashed the bananas in sweet milk and when she didn't have the milk, she'd chew the bananas herself first to make it easier for the boy to swallow. She had the money in a cup in the back of a cupboard, and when they had company the bananas would be hidden in the storage space under the bed. It was clearly understood that no one was to see the bananas. And the money he had received for the sheep was not supposed to be used for anything else.

Later he had taken another sheep from the same farmer's field and sold it to the same man in the Honnesteech in Drachten. He didn't get what the sheep was worth, and it was a dangerous undertaking, but that's how they managed to pull the boy through. When he was five years old, one could hardly tell anymore that he'd had a bad start.

"Pretty good," said Hindrik, when he saw the boy, and in Geeske's opinion it was nothing less than a miracle.

"He's got to be better off than us in the future," Gryt said to him, and that became the next goal.

It was for the boy's sake that he took that job as supervisor on the polder.

Dad had shown him the door. He said: "I'm done with you. I want no slavedriver walking the floor of my house."

Hindrik too wanted to have nothing to do with him.

But it was all for the boy's sake.

And when he fired that lazy pig with the big mouth, Harm Dam, at the insistence of the chairman, that was all for the boy's sake too. And for no other reason.

9.
The
Cigarette
Lighter

The man in the fancy room said: "What do you think, shall we try one more time?"

He looked first at the large desk where he saw a few things that had come from his boy's pocket. He said: "What have you done with him?"

"We've done nothing with him."

The man stood up. "We wanted to hear your story first, and if that's satisfactory . . ."

"Didn't he say anything?"

It wasn't his custom to interrupt.

The man said: "We haven't asked him anything yet."

"Why not?"

"He's young. We'd rather talk with people who have more of a sense of responsibility. Such young fellows don't even know what it's all about, so we protect them as long as possible."

Fear took hold of him again. Something's wrong, they're trying to trap me, he thought to himself. But he said: "I must talk to him first."

"That's odd. You've always let him be, and now all of a sudden you need to talk to him."

"That's just it. He goes his own way, he doesn't tell me anything. That's why I have to ask him first and then I'll let you know."

"I can't allow that."

"Why not?"

The man came out from behind his desk and started pacing the floor. He laughed softly and said: "I've never experienced anything this crazy. You're reversing the roles, you're interrogating me."

He stopped and folded his hands behind his back. "But I can take it from you, isn't that something? I have a weakness for you, that must be it. Just the same, I'm in charge here and I can't allow two suspects to confer together on what their explanation is going to be; that would certainly be unique in investigative practice."

The man had to laugh about it himself.

"But if he was with the others, at that incident last night . . ."

"He was with them. Otherwise we wouldn't have caught him, right?"

"I don't know about that. It happened on the lake, I understand, and he often pokes around there. He's fishing on my license, and at this time of year he often poaches. That's not legal, of course, but . . ."

"Our people do not pick up people for poaching. When we pick up people, it's for other reasons."

"He could've just happened to roam around there."

"You know better."

"No, I don't, and that's why I need to talk to him."

"He was caught with the weapons in his hands."

He tried to imagine it, but since he had seen that tobacco case and the other things, he felt a bit confused. He said: "It looks strange to me."

Then he remembered something. "We have an old shotgun, it was my dad's, and he sometimes takes off with that. We don't have a permit for it, but . . ."

"It wasn't a shotgun but an English stengun, an automatic pistol."

He knew at once that the man was trying to pull a fast one on him. "I wouldn't know what the boy would want a thing like that for. You can't shoot game with something like that, I know that much. What do you want to do with that kind of gun on the lake?"

"You tell me."

He was going to lose this one, so he didn't say any more.

"Your son and several of his cohorts were caught red-handed with the weapons."

"He's not that dumb. Did they shoot with them?"

"They resisted arrest."

He couldn't believe it. He was sure the man was still trying to trick him. "You always lose when you do that."

"You're right about that."

"It's impossible."

He tried to dismiss it, but he was afraid that it was possible. "I did see the water police this spring mess around with containers that had been dropped from air-planes during the night. At least that's what they said."

"Exactly, and those containers had weapons in them, which you know very well."

"I didn't know that, but the police did search my boat."

"And never found anything, of course."

"What would I do with that junk. If I had found some, I would've left them there. Now if it was a good trap . . ."

He got himself pretty well under control again. He didn't know what had happened, but he had a notion that it was different from what the man tried to tell him.

"My boy is not so crazy that he would take on the police and the Germans over a couple of containers full of weapons."

"It wasn't about weapons this time, but about people. Important people who at all costs were not supposed to fall into our hands. But you know nothing about that, right?"

"No, I know nothing about that. What do you mean, about people?"

"You never noticed that yesterday a group of people in a big scow were drifting around on your side of the lake? They spent the whole day there, you know."

"There are plenty of places to hide, so if those people didn't want to be seen, it would be very simple to just pull into the reeds a while when they saw me coming."

"You didn't know either, of course, that day before yesterday three of those persons were in town several times. Everybody saw them and talked about it, but you didn't know it."

"I already told you that I seldom go to town. I'm always home. I don't need other people. What did those people want in town and on the lake?"

"You're doing the questioning again, but go ahead. Those people were supposed to be picked up by an airplane during the night and taken to England. A group of people from around here were supposed to help them with that."

"And you're telling me that Germ was with them?"

"He was with them. And now it's time to do business."

"I've got to talk to him first."

"That's impossible, and now I'm going to tell you exactly how things stand. I want you to make a confession right now, otherwise we'll have to take care of your boy. That means that you likely will not see him again. Are you listening carefully? Then you will not see him again."

"Why won't I see him again?"

"For this sort of thing you get the death penalty, everybody knows that."

"And he won't get that if I tell you a thing or two?"

122

"That is to say, we can then take his age into account. Officially he deserves the death penalty because he was caught with the weapons on him, but you can save him. We're allowed to do that in exceptional cases. We are more interested in the ringleaders, who while safe behind the scenes incite the people to terrorist activity, than in the fools who have to do the dirty work."

He tried to maintain his composure and let the man's words sink in. It was possible that Germ participated in such adventures.

He said: "I don't know the people. If Germ was with them, he should know more about it. That's why I have to talk to him first."

At that moment he became unsure again. The boy's tobacco case lay there, and his pocketknife and the lighter.

"I've gotta talk to him first, I wanta see him."

The man did not answer. He took a cigarette and searched for a light. When he felt his pockets in vain, he took Germ's lighter and tried to use it. The thing wouldn't work, as usual. The man flicked it several times and inspected it. When he put it down, he took his handkerchief and wiped his hands.

He took a step forward and looked at the spot where the cigarette lighter had lain. A few drops of water had spattered on the desk. He took another step forward and took the tobacco case. He opened it; the tobacco was soaked.

The man said: "Leave it alone," and got up.

He looked at the man. He looked him right in the eye, and then he understood.

He put the case down and at the same time grabbed the man by the chest with his free hand and jerked him halfway across the desk. Then with his other hand he grabbed him by the throat and squeezed hard.

When the soldier jumped him, he staggered backward. He now had both hands around the man's throat and squeezed still harder. He still held the man in his grip when the soldier hit him over the head with the butt of his rifle.

10.
This
Is
Enough

Later it was hard for him to place the events in the right sequence.

First they dragged him through the corridor. He came to when they were halfway up the stairs, and began to scream. He kicked and flailed away so that they had to release him momentarily. A soldier rammed him in the stomach with the butt of his gun, and he fell forward on the stone floor. They bent his arms back and two men stepped on his legs. Then they had him under control.

"A hard head," a soldier panted. "I really thought I had beat his brains out."

The other said: "There's something wrong with his brain all right. It's all scrambled."

Later on he remembered this, but after he heard the soldier say there was something wrong with his brain, he lost consciousness again. He came to on top of a table on which they had laid him. Both of his legs were tied down, and they had also tied a rope across his stomach, but he was able to move his upper torso.

He said aloud to himself: "I hope I strangled him."

People came to see him and one of them said: "It looks to me like he's calmed down pretty well."

A man bent over him and said: "Still a little light-headed, I suppose? That will last a while yet. But you carried on like a madman."

It wasn't the same man as the one in the fancy room, but this one was dressed as a civilian too, and spoke Frisian.

Maybe it was the suit that brought everything back. The truth of the situation hit him with such a bewildering force that he couldn't stand it and began to scream again. He yelled that it wasn't possible, or something like that. At least that's what the other one told him later. He had heard him right through all the walls.

Then there was nothing for a while. Sometimes there was the shadow of a soldier who stuffed a rag in his mouth and thereby muffled his screams.

"It must've been an awful mess," the man in the cell said later. "The whole place was jumping. I think they almost panicked. I could hear what sounded like at least five soldiers running through the hallway. And all that, I think, was because of you."

The world came back to him piece by piece. First he heard voices. The ordinary voices of people talking together. In between was the ticking of the typewriters just like that morning in the city hall. The voices and the ticking came from the room next to where he lay on the table. The door was open.

He lay on the table and sensed that he was tied down. He didn't open his eyes to see how things were. He didn't move either, because he was afraid that would alert attention.

At first that was all. He knew he was alive and that there were people nearby. He had to get used to it, but before he managed, other things came between. It was a strange vision: He saw the other man in the cell who said that he didn't have a stomachache anymore.

Right afterward he suddenly felt a great sorrow that overwhelmed him. He moaned, and someone came immediately to his side. He became afraid and he lay motionless, with his eyes closed. Fortunately, the man left again.

I won't be able to hold myself together, he thought. It's going to hit me in a moment, and then I'll go crazy.

"You were gone for only a few hours," the other man in the cell said later.

He had the feeling that it had been days, but the man must be right, for soon after the soldier came with supper—two slices of dark bread and a mug of water for each.

When he lay on the bunk with his jacket under his head, just like that morning, he said aloud: "He's all through now and he didn't suffer much."

He had asked the man about it who stood by the table.

"Shot in flight," said the man. "Your son jumped out of the scow and swam toward the reeds. He shouldn't have done that."

He knew that this man spoke the truth. Germ wouldn't have let himself get caught easily and he could swim like a water rat. He wanted to reach the marshes, where no one could have caught up with him. Except the bullet.

"It didn't have to happen," added the man. "If he had let himself get caught, we likely would've sent him to Germany. But he tried to escape and that is the dumbest thing you can do in a situation like that."

The man seemed sensible. He talked about a heavy blow, especially when it's an only child.

"But you have to go on," said the man. "You still have a wife and you have your work."

The man also told him that he was going to put him back in the cell with the other prisoner in order to recover.

He would have much preferred to be alone. He had to keep telling himself that the boy was finished now and that he hadn't suffered. Shot in the back and killed instantly. He hadn't suffered. That last realization gave him a bit of relief.

"Germ is finished," he said. "It's all over, and I don't have to worry about him anymore."

The man below him said something, but he wasn't listening.

"I'm through with everything," he said again.

He reflected on that and found it was exactly so: He was through with everything.

"I've had so much work with him, and Gryt has too. I feel sorry for her, because she had to go through just as much for him as I did, a lot more even. It started before he was born."

He thought it over.

"And then just like that it's all over. I've always been afraid of it. I always expected it, really, but not like this. I always sorta figured that he might get into an accident some day. During the first few years I thought that one day he would just die because he was such a weak little kid. But that went better than expected. Those two sheep pulled him through, because without bananas he would've never made it. Gryt and I said to each other: If we can only get him in good health first."

His head was hurting. There were clots of blood in his hair.

"They sure worked you over," the other man said after they brought him back to the cell.

When he told him that the boy had been shot and killed, the man grew pale.

"Shot dead, damn . . . . Do they do that here?"

"Last night on the lake, they shot him just like that because he tried to get away. And now it's over. He's finished and I'm finished. And he didn't suffer, that's a

130

good thing. One time I hauled a boy out from underneath the ice. He must've struggled quite a while to get out. He had foam on his mouth. That's terrible. Many a night I saw that awful twisted face before me. A bullet makes a quick end. He probably never even knew what hit him."

He lay there reflecting.

"We all have to go sometime, the one sooner than the other. But what difference does it really make. I remember exactly how that first hit me. I must've been seven or eight when I discovered that life is terminal, that we are mortal. Up to then I had no idea of that. I was much too busy fishing for bass in the Bonne pools. But then Brant Hoen died, our neighbor. How was that possible? Well, Mom said, everybody has to die sometime. Me too, Mom? You too. That did it. I didn't feel like doing anything anymore. I didn't even care to go fishing for bass anymore. If you were going to die anyway, why bother with anything. Of course you get over that, but not all the way. I've always known that life doesn't have much purpose."

The man below said: "I don't know what you're rambling on about, but it's pretty awful. I'm gonna give up, come what may."

He didn't touch his food. The other man ate his too.

Right after suppertime, the man in civilian clothes entered, accompanied by two soldiers.

He did not rise but gave them a sideways look from his bunk. The men stood next to him, but he turned his face away and looked at the wall.

"Are you able to be questioned? Yes, I'm sorry, but we have our work to do. I should tell you first, though, that your son's body reposes in the village police station. He

can't stay there, of course. They can take the remains to
your home and then there will still be all kinds of opportunity for you to make the necessary arrangements. They
released the corpse already, and if you're in a condition
to make a statement, we'll release you immediately and
then you can go ahead and do the things that in such cir-
cumstances have to be done."

He said: "I'm sure they'll take care of things."

"Yes, of course, but maybe you belong to a burial
society, you would know that better than I."

"Let's leave it at that, then," he said.

"What do you mean, don't you want to be there yourself?"

"He's dead, isn't he?"

The man paused a moment. "What did you say?"

"He's dead, isn't he?"

"Well, yes, of course. I'm just trying to be helpful. But
it's up to you. Why don't you get up and come along
with me, then."

"Do I have to be interrogated again?"

"Yes, I'm afraid that can't be helped."

He didn't move. He said: "I don't want to see that
man again, that man in the fancy room."

"You won't see him again. This is another
department."

"I'll kill that man."

"You almost killed him already. That wasn't so smart,
though I can understand your reaction. It wasn't our
intent to give you that information. We wanted to spare
you."

He rose, and the shaking started again; he felt it
coming.

"I had to find that out for myself. First you murder

132

my boy and then you use him to pump information out of me."

He lashed out, but his arms were heavy and instead of grabbing the man by the throat, he dropped his arms and started to weep. His crying was brief, but it stopped the shaking.

He said with emphasis on each word: "What beasts you are. I thought I knew your kind. The Royal Police have often manhandled me, and the cops too. And I always thought that nobody was meaner than judges and other big wheels, but you're it. Worse bastards than you don't exist. You go in cahoots with the Germans and you do their dirty work for them."

The man said abruptly: "Along to the office."

The Germans grabbed him by his shoulders and pulled him off the bunk. He was no longer tempted to resist. He said only: "You'll not get a word out of me."

"We will see about that," said the man.

He felt very sure of himself. When they put him on his feet next to the bunk, he straightened his back in spite of the pain and walked ahead of the soldiers with great dignity. They took him to a bare room that had nothing but a chair in it. The man sat down on the chair, and the soldiers placed him right in front of it. They stood on either side of him and placed their hands on his shoulders.

The man said: "It seems to me you've experienced enough today. I'll give you a good half hour to get a hold of yourself. No longer than that, because the people we're after have had too much time already to make their getaway. We intend to make another raid tonight to try to capture the ringleaders. And before we do that we need the names. From you and from no one else. You have fifteen minutes to write down the names and addresses. Here's paper and pencil."

He did not accept it.

"Fine. In fifteen minutes you come back here and then I'll write them down."

They took him back to his cell. The other man stood doubled up by the barrel and asked: "Do you really intend to say nothing? You really know nothing about it?"

"I know a little, but I won't tell 'em a thing," he said.

"You won't have to tell 'em much, maybe one name will be enough."

"I could give them one name, but the man never did anything to me. He's a real dud, with an orange ribbon under his lapel. And he's a coward to boot, otherwise he wouldn't be hiding that ribbon."

"What's he doing in the underground!"

"He looks after people who need a place to hide and Jews and so on, and when airplanes come with weapons, he goes into action then too."

"So that guy is responsible for sending your son to his death. What in the world holds you back, man?"

That he was responsible for sending Germ to his death was not true. The boy did not let himself be told. He had never told Germ anything. The girl had egged him on, maybe, but he could take it from her. And he was already involved with those men before he had met her. He had nothing against the girl, and he had always liked her. A nervous wreck, said Gryt. A hot number, Willem said later. She'd like to crawl right into Germ's pants sometimes. According to Gryt the girl had no shame, and she looked with disapproval at the way the girl would run in her panties to the water pump in the morning. He looked at her often, but in a different way.

And when he slept in the back of the house in summertime, he'd wait for Germ and the girl to go to the attic.

"Are you sleeping again?"

The man stood next to him. He opened his eyes and shook his head.

"I've not had to bury a child yet," said the man. "I don't know what that's like, but it seems terrible to me. I want to get outta here so bad. If it makes no difference to you, aren't you willing to help me?"

"Then maybe I'll help you get out, but somebody else get in," he said. "I can't help you."

"You mean I'm worse than that man? You said yourself that he was a dud. Maybe you don't like me either, but I'm standing before you."

"I have nothing against you. I don't know you, and I really don't know the other man either, so that's about the same. But he's about the same age as you, and I think he still has some young kids, just like you."

"But if it makes no difference, then . . ."

The man kept on whining about it, but he gave no answer. After a good quarter of an hour the soldiers returned. They took him back to the bare room, but now they placed him on the chair and the men stood around him. They looked down on him and told him he couldn't get up.

"You've already lost your son," said the man. "If you want to risk your own life as well . . ."

"That's exactly why," he said calmly.

"Sure, you blame us for the death of your son, and now out of revenge you refuse to speak. But don't you want to go back to your wife and your fishing?"

"This is enough," he said.

The man didn't understand that. "I don't believe you realize that it's going to turn out bad for you."

"But I said that this is enough."

"Don't you want your freedom back?"

"I'm not interested in it."

"That we will have to see," said the man.

He signaled to the soldiers; he himself went out.

The soldiers began to beat him, not hard, but in sensitive areas. It was only for a short while and then the man came back. He said: "This is just a taste. What do you say now?"

He sat straight up in the chair and said nothing.

"Answer me!" yelled the man.

He was tired of all the talk, and when he spoke it was more for himself than for the others. He said: "So often I've had to do things against my will, now I'm going to quit. It's not necessary anymore."

He was dense, that man. He kept on asking and became increasingly angry. He kept leaving and then the soldiers would start beating him again. At first he deflected the beatings with his hands and arms, but he fell off the chair, and when he lay on the floor they kicked him. But the beatings never lasted long, and it was clear that the soldiers held back.

The man returned and said: "This is just the beginning. You will now get another fifteen minutes and then it's going to get more serious."

The soldiers took him back to his cell.

11.
That's What
I Had
Always
Wanted

It became increasingly apparent to him how things really stood. In fact, he marveled how clear it all was to him now.

I never really wanted to, he thought, I've done everything against my will, my whole life long. It started with Gryt, and it never stopped until this morning, this afternoon.

That's the way it was, and he had always thought it couldn't be any other way. In the first place, he couldn't abandon Gryt. He who dances must pay the piper, was Dad's saying, and that's what everybody did who got a girl in trouble. It was the right thing to do.

He felt sorry for Gryt. She'd been just as crazy about the boy as he. She must be having a very hard time right now.

If I could be with her now, would that be of help to her? he asked himself. He knew the answer. He wouldn't even dare put a hand on her shoulder. He hoped that she would be well taken care of.

They shouldn't have had the boy. If he had died as a baby, they wouldn't miss him anymore now and it would have changed things in so many ways for them. He could've gone to America without bowing to anybody. That he had to take a shot at the forest ranger for the boy's sake wasn't so bad. The trip to the relief office in Beets was much harder. He hated himself when he went to the store with that note to get baby food. And when he waited for the liter of milk at the farmer's in Aldbeets, his body ached from annoyance.

The old man simply rejected a handout and let Mom die. And Bareld had given him a beating for that when he left for America.

The girl had not really understood when he told her that story.

"I think that's terrible," she said, "to beat up your dad just like that."

"Not just like that; according to him, Dad had it coming."

"Why did he have to do it on the day he left for America?"

"Well, that was his last chance. He must've suppressed it, you know. He kept it inside, but he wanted to let Dad know that he'd done wrong."

"Why didn't you talk about it?"

"At our place such things were never talked about."

"Was your dad really so bad?"

"Dad was proud, he always had to be right, and if you disagreed with him he'd get mad."

"And then he'd hit you."

"Yeah, then he'd beat us. But when we got bigger we'd stand up to him."

"Did you hit him too before you left home?"

"No, I didn't want to do that. Dad was a proud man, he didn't know how to be different. And he was a free socialist, he was very high on that. When Domela Nieuwenhuis came for a talk and anyone should so much as point at the man, Dad would have conniptions. They never bothered Domela when he came to our area. But I'll bet you Dad would've taken care of any policeman who'd give Domela a hard time. That would've been worth ten years in the slammer to him. Dad wasn't sensible. And that kind will forget their family at such times, they lose all sense of responsibility. And that's not right."

The girl was thinking. "I believe you do admire your Dad a bit for that."

"Not at all. Dad was not a good man, everybody knows that in Beets."

Then the girl wanted to know how they happened to leave Beets.

"Did you have trouble?" she asked.

Because Germ had told her that real Beetsters would never leave except if they'd had trouble, like Germ and Bareld.

What would a boy like Germ know about that? He said something to the effect that they weren't exactly a close family, and that was true. He would've liked to tell her that it was because of Harm Dam, the one he had to fire, but he didn't get to that.

It was when he was supervisor on the polder. Harm Dam was a lousy worker. Always a big mouth and letting others do all the work. Some said he was absolutely right in firing Harm. But it wasn't his idea. He had noticed that with the dredging of the underground canal, Koene Vaartjes hauled twice as much mud as did Harm Dam, while Harm was in twice as good a physical condition. Koene worked his tail off, but he wanted another partner because now they couldn't nearly manage to make their cubic meter quota. And that was all because of Harm, who was forever stopping to refill his pipe.

"If you don't do it, then I'll have to do it next week," the company chairman said. Later Gryt said the same thing, and she was right. Workers like Harm Dam were worthless and you couldn't defend them.

That's what he said to Dad and Hindrik too, but they never set foot in his house again.

He stared into the air vent, which didn't let much light in anymore.

He said aloud: "They were right, of course, Dad and Hindrik. What's the difference how many cubic meters of mud you load onto the boat in a day. It's about something else altogether."

"What are you talking about," said the other man. He was pacing the cell, all bent over. Now and again he lifted the right leg and let a fart and then kept pacing.

He said: "I'd like you not to talk."

For there were still many things for him to ponder.

It had all been for the boy's sake. Gryt and he had come to a firm agreement that the boy must have a better life than they had. That's why he had let himself get talked into taking that job in the polder. Not a high but a steady income, and that was worth a lot. Gryt would be able to save some, and if the boy might have some plans someday, they'd be able to help him out and get started.

"He should get a good education," said Gryt. "Maybe we can send him to high school."

"We shouldn't reach too high. A trade school would be good enough."

That was fine with Gryt. Carpentry should make a good living, she thought.

"You have to have some stability," said the man in Beets. "That wandering from one thing to another doesn't suit you either. You're able to do better."

He knew very well what was behind that talk, and Hindrik said it in so many words: "There, now they got rid of you."

They hadn't offered that kind of job to Hindrik. He did make a lot of noise, but they didn't have as much trouble with Hindrik as they had with him. He didn't give in as quickly as the others.

At that meeting at Three Corners in Lippenhuizen, he was the first to get hit because he was the one to go after the police all by himself. When they went on strike, his houseboat was watched and they took his old bike so that he couldn't go to Jobbega to get the workers to strike there. Twice he had been in charge of roll call and in Beets had been the spokesman more than once when a group of them held a demonstration in city hall.

Gryt said he was his own worst enemy. He caused all the trouble, he got the most beatings, and when it was all over, he was locked out while the others could go back to work. Gryt was right.

He fired Harm Dam, but he told the chairman of the company the next day that he wanted to quit. That had made Gryt furious too, and she was right again. Four weeks without work and absolute poverty because he refused to go to Hindrik or to Dad for help. And finally the little shack on the lake and still more poverty. Until the autumn of '39 when he got the knack of it and began to catch a lot more fish.

"All for the boy's sake," he said, "and I never really wanted to. This is peculiar, but I know exactly now what I did want."

First, though, he had to straighten out a few more things in his mind. That incident in Germany, for example. They must've been working on the railroad at the time because every week they'd be somewhere else. It had been Douwe Krist's idea. He had found himself a girl and said that this was his kind of woman. "If I want to get married someday, I'll get me one from Germany, " he said.

But for the time being this would do.

"We make a nice Sunday evening of it: we sit in the cafe a while with the girls, and then we head for the fields. Without too much fuss—pants off and go to it. And never any of that whining, like: Do we have to do it again so soon? Of course not, the more often the better."

"Were you ever in Germany?" he asked the other man in the cell.

"Not I, and I don't look forward to it either. It's s'posed to be pretty bad in those camps. They talked about Amersfoort. Do they want to send you to Germany?"

"No, I don't mean that. I was there in the '20s and '30s, mostly in wintertime, but if there was no work at home then sometimes during the summer too. I had a woman there I'd like to have stayed with."

"I wish you'd talk about something else," said the other. "Women is the last thing I need right now. And it would be better to think about your own wife; right now she must need you pretty bad."

"That's never been the case. I've had a great house-keeper in her. She can really keep things together, she's very good at that. I haven't slept with her in years."

Dad had said it more than once: With Hindrik every shot is a hit, and you only have one, and even that was a mistake. I don't get it, a big fleshy woman like Gryt, do you mount her often enough?

Geart Heida said that too when the two of them were at the fair in Beets. "Why don't you try it with that girl with the big buns, that's something to grab onto."

Geart arranged it with Gryt's girlfriend, whom he said

later had put out that very same night. According to
Geart, he could easily have scored with Gryt, too, if he
only handled it right. And so he made a few more runs.
But he probably would never have succeeded if the four
of them hadn't had too much brandy at the fair in
Gorredijk. Later that night they landed in the haymow of
the farm where the other girl worked, and Gryt had to
play along if she didn't want to be a spoilsport.

A mistake, Dad said later.

A bad mistake, even though he didn't realize it at the
time. He had sex, as they called it, when he felt like it,
but not often because Gryt didn't want it very often.
She'd rather not have it at all.

The girl in Germany was different. They were sluts
really, said Douwe Krist.

That kind of slut I would've liked to have, he
thought. As often as I lay waiting in the back of the
house for Germ and the girl, that's as often as I thought
about it. The kind of girl Willem described as one who
just about crawls inside your pants. One who's pretty
easy to talk to, enjoys sex, and is not scared of life. That's
the kind I would've liked to have kids with and I
wouldn't have worried about it, not with that kind of
woman.

And I've always wanted to oppose everything, just
like Dad. I really wanted to be against the Germans. And
once we'd gotten rid of them, and others like that
rightist schoolteacher with the orange ribbon got into
power, then we'd start all over again. Because our kind
of people are meant to be rebels. It's always been that
way and that's how it'll stay. Our kind thrives under
repression.

"And that's what I had always wanted," he said aloud.

"You can go to hell as far as I'm concerned," said the other man. "Damn it, I sure wish I was outta here. Why don't you help me, man."

The soldiers stood by the bunk and when he didn't get up quickly enough, they yanked him off.

The man in the bare room tried one more time. "Use your senses, man."

They beat him again. The man stayed too and kept yelling, "Confess, you must confess." The man worked himself into a sweat.

At last they put him down on the chair again to recover.

The man was gone for five minutes. When he returned, he said: "You will now go to the other side, to the specialists. We call that a stiffer interrogation. But you can still get out of it."

They pulled him up; the man stood in the door. "Well, are we going to get something?"

He said: "Go to hell, you bastard."

He wanted to kick him in the belly, but the soldiers yanked him back.

They dragged him through the corridor and he didn't see the man again.

Later, after each torture session, they asked him if he was about ready to confess. At first he lashed out, but they soon overpowered him. He was tied down and then all he could do was scream.

They shot him early in the morning on the outskirts of Leeuwarden, at the same time as the other prisoner who had seen too much and therefore also had to be executed, though he never understood why.

146

But he did.

He saw how they let the other man walk on ahead and then shot him in the back of the head, and he heard as they came his way afterward.

He also saw the beginning of dawn on the horizon. Other days at this time he'd be out on the lake.

He would very much like to know where the girl was right now. He did hope that Gryt would keep the child with her.